MOUNTAIN DIRE

EAST

for

Truckers, RV, and Motorhome Drivers

Locations
and Descriptions of
over 300 Mountain Passes and
Steep Grades in Eleven Eastern States

Acknowledgments

A word of thanks must be extended to all of the people who helped during the gathering of information for **Mountain Directory West** and **Mountain Directory East**. Highway Patrol officers and Department of Transportation employees in twenty-two states were always helpful and informative about where to find the longest and steepest hills. Because of the enormous area covered by **Mountain Directory West** and **Mountain Directory East**, it is inevitable that some grades have been missed. Please write or call if you are aware of grades that should be included in the books. This type of information is most welcome and will be passed along. Address and phone number below.

All the color relief maps in these publications were made with Cartesia® Software of Lambertville, NJ.

To order additional copies of these books please call **1-800-594-5999** or visit our website at
www.mountaindirectory.com
or send us an e-mail at
mtndir@earthlink.net

Mountain Directory West and **Mountain Directory East** are published by:
R&R Publishing Inc.
PO Box 941
Baldwin City, KS 66006-0941
1-800-594-5999

ISBN: 0-9776290-1-5 **Mountain Directory West** © Copyright 2006
ISBN: 0-9776290-0-7 **Mountain Directory East** © Copyright 2006

INTRODUCTION

There is an old saying among over-the-road truckers. "There are two kinds of drivers--those who've been in trouble on a mountain grade, and those who will be." Unfortunately, this also applies to many RVers. Trucks and RVs have similar problems regarding weight, engine power, and braking in mountainous terrain.

Imagine yourself descending a mountain grade in your RV. You didn't know there was such a long, steep grade on this highway. What a surprise! And things are not going well. You have a white-knuckle grip on the steering wheel. The engine is not holding back all of this weight, the brakes are smelling hot or even smoking, you're pushing harder on the brake pedal but your speed keeps increasing. All you can see ahead is more mountain. Your mind is racing through all of the available options and none of them are good. "I've got to do something," you say "or I'm not going to make it." The options include: run into the rock wall, go over the side, hit those trees, or see if you can make the next curve and ride it out. You choose the last option and, if you are lucky, you make it to the bottom in one piece. You pull over and while you are waiting for your heart to stop pounding, you wipe the sweat from your face and you notice your shirt is soaked, your mouth is dry, and your hands are shaking. You are thinking, *"If I had known it was going to be like that............"*

Perhaps your rig has difficulty during the steep climbs. The temperature is in the 90's and the grade is so steep that you can barely climb it in first gear. The engine and transmission temperatures are rising. How far to the top of this hill? You don't know if it's one mile or ten. Something smells hot. What to do? Pull over and cool off? But then all momentum is lost. Can you even get started again? You wish you had unhooked the car you're dragging up this hill behind the motorhome. If you are lucky, you can do that next time. You are wondering how many thousand dollars a new engine and transmission will be.

During the last few years we have heard many stories about very expensive repairs to drive train components. Sometimes rigs are lost entirely. A highway patrol officer in Oregon told us that in the summer an average of one motorhome per week burns to the ground while trying to climb Cabbage Hill on I-84 east of Pendleton. If a fire starts, the nearest fire department is likely to be many miles away. By the time they arrive, there is nothing left to do but hose down the ashes.

Since 1993 we have been collecting and publishing information about mountain passes and steep grades. Combined, **Mountain Directory West** and **Mountain Directory East** give the locations and descriptions of over 700 mountain passes and steep grades in 22 states. This is vital information for anyone driving a large or heavy vehicle. The Mountain Directory books tell you where the steep grades are, how long they are, how steep (%) they are, whether the road is two lane, three lane, or four lane, if there are escape ramps, switchbacks, sharp curves, speed limits, etc. With this information, one can know ahead of time what a pass is like and make an informed decision about whether to go over or around. If you decide to go over, perhaps the cool morning hours would ease the strain on the engine and transmission during the climb. Unhooking the towed vehicle would make the climb and the descent easier. Knowing what lies ahead is half the battle.

Many people are under the impression that the grades in the eastern mountains are not as serious as the grades in the western mountains. Apparently this is because the elevations are not as high in the eastern states. But elevation alone is not the problem--it is the *change in elevation* that makes a grade potentially hazardous. If all other factors are equal, a grade that descends from 4000' to 1000' over 10 miles is no different than a grade that descends from 10000' to 7000' over 10 miles. Either way you have a 3000' change in elevation spread over 10 miles. (This example would result in an average grade of almost 6% for 10 miles.)

A large percentage of the grades in the western states are in the 6% range. A large percentage of the grades in the eastern states are 8, 9, or 10% and sometimes even more. The eastern grades are often shorter but this is not always so. A quick glance through this book will reveal over 50 grades that are between 7 and 10% and from 4 to 7 miles long. There are others that are even more challenging. The road to the top of Whiteface Mountain in New York is 8 to 10% for 8 miles. There would be no need for truckers to use this road but RVs are allowed. Near Cumberland, Maryland there is a hill on I-68 that is posted as 6% for 13 miles. In North Carolina highway 181 crosses the Blue Ridge Parkway and the southbound descent is 11 miles of grade that varies from 6 to 10%. Much of it is 8 to 9%. These grades are just as hazardous as the grades in the western states.

While every effort has been made to ensure the accuracy of the maps included in this book, it is nearly impossible to include all necessary detail on such small pages. We recommend that these maps be used in conjunction with larger, more detailed road maps.

In most cases the passes and hills are described as descents. In other words, a pass will be described from the summit down in one direction and then from the summit down in the other direction. This directory does not claim to include every steep grade. In fact, because of the enormous area we have tried to cover, we can guarantee that we have probably missed some. Sometimes the percentages quoted are estimates and many times they are based on road signs or information provided by highway departments. This book does not attempt to rate passes or grades according to difficulty. There is an enormous variety in vehicles and equipment. A hill that is very difficult for one vehicle may be no problem at all for a similar vehicle that is equipped differently. Driver judgment is critical in deciding which hills should be avoided.

The purpose of this book is not to discourage drivers from going where they please. It is only to inform them of the conditions they may encounter and to encourage them to make sure their equipment is in good repair. Brakes must be in good working order and properly adjusted and the engine and transmission should be used to slow the vehicle whenever possible, thus saving the brakes and keeping them cool enough to retain their stopping power. The engine's cooling system should be in good repair to prevent overheating during the climbs. Turning off the air conditioner during climbs may help, and if necessary, turning on the heater will help dissipate heat from the engine.

There are many aftermarket devices that can help heavy vehicles in the mountains. Some will help by increasing horsepower for the climbs. These include turbos and exhaust systems. Other devices, such as engine braking systems can help during the descents. Some products, like gear splitters and auxiliary transmissions can help during the climbs and the descents. Many of these products also improve fuel economy (while delivering more horsepower) and reduce wear and tear on the drive train.

The main ingredients involved in overheated brakes are the length of the grade, the steepness of the grade, and the speed and weight of the vehicle. Reducing any of these will improve the chances of getting down the mountain without overheating the brakes. Most of the time, the only one the driver can change is speed. Reducing speed may keep you alive. Remember the old phrase, *"You can go down a mountain a thousand times too slowly, but only once too fast."*

The majority of the mountains in the eastern United States are found within the area outlined by the dashed lines on the map below. The White Mountains are in New Hampshire, the Green Mountains are in Vermont, and the Adirondacks and Catskills are in New York. The Alleghenies are in Pennsylvania and West Virginia, the Blue Ridge Mountains are in Virginia and North Carolina, the Cumberlands are in Kentucky and Tennessee, and the Great Smoky Mountains are along the Tennessee-North Carolina border. Collectively, these mountain ranges make up what is known as the Appalachian Mountains, which stretch from northern Alabama to the Gaspe Peninsula in Quebec.

VT

NH

NY

MA

PA

WV

MD

KY

VA

TN

NC

CONTENTS

(States are listed from North to South.)

VERMONT

1   **Vermont highway 108** *(from Stowe to Jeffersonville, VT. (called Smuggler's Notch)*

As soon as you turn onto 108 from highway 100 in Stowe, you will see a sign stating **"Not a through route for tractor trailers."** The climb to the top of Smuggler's Notch doesn't begin until about 5 miles farther west. At this point the grade increases to **7-10%** for almost a mile and then the highway rolls up and down for about 2½ miles. At this point more signs appear: **"Steep and narrow road with sharp curves"** and **"Road ahead unsafe for trailers, trucks, and busses"** and **"Tractor trailers prohibited."** The road narrows so much that they didn't paint a center line and there is little shoulder.

From this point to the top of the pass is only about a mile but the grade varies between **10 and 15% with extremely sharp and narrow hairpin turns.** During one of these hairpins the grade increases to probably **20%**. Yes it's short, but if you must stop due to traffic or you can't pull the grade, you may have to back down the hill. It gets better! Just before you get to the top, the road narrows to one lane during a hairpin turn that curves around a large boulder. You can't see traffic coming down the hill because of the boulder so you must sneak around it hoping no one is coming.

The descent down the north side toward Jeffersonville is narrow and winding but does not include the sharp switchbacks found on the south side. The grade is still quite steep, beginning with a very short section of **10-12%** near the top, followed by **3 miles** of descent that varies from **6 to 10%** with the last mile a **steady 8%**. After this steep section the roadway rolls up and down for almost 4 miles and then descends at about **7%** for the last half mile into Jeffersonville.

2   **Vermont highway 242** *(between Jay and Montgomery Center, VT.)*

The top of this grade is about midway between Jay and the junction of 242 and 118 near Montgomery Center. The westbound descent towards Montgomery Center begins with a steep grade sign and grade that varies from **12% to 8%** for about ½ mile and then eases to 6%. The road then stair steps down for the next 6 miles with short sections of steep grade alternating with sections of flat or mild grade. The last mile before reaching the junction is all descent that varies from **8 to 11%**.

The eastbound descent toward Jay also begins with a steep grade warning sign and about ½ mile of **12%** grade. The descent is interrupted for a ½ mile 6% climb and then continues with a sign reading "Steep winding hill" and 30 mph curves. The grade is **6 to 8% for the next 4 miles** with only a couple of short sections of mild grade and a ½ mile section of **12%** grade just before reaching Jay.

3   **Vermont highway 105** *(between highway 101 and Richford, VT.)*

The top of this grade is about 5 miles west of the junction with 101. The eastbound descent (toward 101) begins with a steep grade warning and about **2 miles of 6 to 7%** grade. The remaining 2 miles of descent include sections of 6 to 7% grade alternating with sections of 4 to 5%. It is a smooth two lane road with 35 mph curves.

The westbound descent toward Richford begins with a steep grade warning and a series of 35 and 40 mph curves. The grade is **steady 6 to 8% for almost 3 miles**. The grade then stair steps down with short sections of 6 to 8% grade alternating with flat spots or mild grade for about 4 miles to the junction of 105A which is about 3½ miles east of Richford.

4 Vermont highway 58 *(between Irasburg and Lowell, VT., highway 58 between Lowell and Montgomery Center, which is known as Hazen's Notch, is not included here because it is almost all gravel.)*

The eastbound descent toward Irasburg begins with a steep grade warning and about one mile of 6 to 7% grade followed by ½ mile of 12% and then ½ mile of 9%.

Starting from the top of this hill and going west there is a ¾ mile 6% descent followed by a ½ mile 6% climb to another peak. At this point there is a steep grade warning and about 2½ miles of 3 to 5% grade followed by about ½ mile of 7% at the bottom of the hill.

5 I-91

I-91 includes many short 6% grades. Few are more than a mile long. One exception is a **4 mile 5-6%** grade between mileposts 146 and 150. This section is just south of Barton, VT. This is a climb for northbound traffic and a descent for southbound traffic.

6 I-93

Between the junction of I-91 and the New Hampshire state line, there are several short 6% grades on I-93, the longest of which is two mile descent that ends at the I-91 junction.

7 US highway 302 *(between Barre and Groton, VT.)*

The highest point on this road seems to be about 6 miles west of Groton. Some sections of this two lane road are quite smooth and wide, and some sections are more ordinary. The eastbound descent toward Groton begins with a sign reading **"Steep grade next 3 miles."** The first ½ mile is about 8% with 40 mph curves. From there to Groton the grade stair steps down with short sections of 5 and 6% alternating with short sections of flat or mild grade. There is one other short section (about ½ mile) of 7 to 8% grade about halfway down the hill. There are numerous 35 mph curves.

The descent toward Barre is similar with short 5 and 6% grades alternating with short stretches of mild or flat grade.

8 Vermont highway 113 *(between I-91 and Chelsea, VT.)*

Upon leaving I-91 and turning west onto 113, one is greeted by a steep grade sign and almost one mile of steady **7%** descent with 40 mph curves. The next 16 miles are rolling hills. The last **3 to 4 miles** into Chelsea are **steady 6 to 7%** descent with 35 mph curves. During the last half mile into Chelsea, the descent becomes steeper, to about **10%**.

9 Vermont highway 64 *(east of I-89 to Williamstown, VT.)*

The sign says **"Steep grade 4 miles--not recommended for trucks."** The grade is indeed steep and the road is narrow, rough and winding. The descent into Williamstown varies from **6% to 10 or 11%** and is **steady** except for a few very short sections of lesser grade.

10 Vermont highway 64 *(west of I-89.)*

This is a very smooth three lane highway (climbing lane on the uphill side) with a ½ mile section of 6% westbound descent near the top. The grade then eases as you pass a sign stating "Steep grade next 2 miles." About a mile later you pass a sign stating **"Runaway truck ramp 1 mile"** and the grade increases to about 6% for ½ mile and then 10% for the last ½ mile. The truck ramp entrance is on the right. Only ¼ mile after the truck ramp there is a stop sign at the junction with highway 12.

11 Roxbury Gap Road *(between Roxbury and Warren, VT.)*

This road is gravel for a couple of miles on either side of the peak. During the gravel section the grade is quite steep, about **10 or 12%** on both sides of the hill with lesser grade below that.

12 Lincoln Gap Road *(between Warren and Lincoln, VT.)*

Upon leaving Warren and starting the westbound ascent of this road, there is a sign stating: **"Not recommended for trailers."** There is a short section of 6-7% climb and then some lesser grade. The pavement turns to gravel for a one mile section. When the pavement returns the grade increases to about **10%** for ½ mile. It then becomes more rough, narrow and winding and the grade increases to **15% or more** for about a mile until you reach the top of the hill. The Long Trail crosses here and the elevation is 2424 feet above sea level.

The descent toward Lincoln begins with switchbacks and **15+%** grade for almost a mile. The gravel returns during this section and lasts for about 1½ miles. The grade eases to **8 or 9%** and then about 5% and then the road begins to stair step down toward Lincoln with two short sections of **12-14%** grade included. The total descent from the top of the hill to Lincoln is about 3½ miles.

13 Vermont highway 17 *(between Bristol and Irasville, VT.)*

This road is posted **"Not recommended for winter travel by trucks, busses, or trailers."** The top of this hill is about 6 miles west of Irasville. The eastbound descent (toward Irasville) begins with about 1½ miles of very steep grade (about **12%**) and continuous sharp switchbacks. The grade then eases to about 10% for almost a mile and then eases to 2 or 3% for the remainder of the trip to Irasville.

The westbound descent also begins with switchbacks and about ½ mile of 12% grade. The grade then varies but is mostly **10% for the next 2½ miles** with constant 25 mph switchbacks. The final seven miles to the junction of highway 116 are rolling hills with some short 6-8% descents included.

14 Vermont highway 125 *(from Hancock to Ripton and East Middlebury, VT.)*

This is a good two lane highway with numerous 25, 35, and 40 mph curves. The top of this hill is about 6 miles west of Hancock. The eastbound descent (toward Hancock) begins with 2 miles of grade that varies from 6 to 10%. The remaining 4 miles to Hancock are rolling hills.

The westbound descent is similar with grade that varies from **6 to 10% for almost 2 miles**. The remaining 4 miles to Ripton are rolling hills. The last ½ mile before reaching East Middlebury is posted at **15%** grade. At the bottom of this hill is a 20 mph curve and a narrow bridge followed by another 20 mph curve.

15 Brandon Gap Road *(on Vermont 73 between Rochester and Brandon, VT.)*

The top of this hill is about 5 miles east of Forest Dale, which is 3 miles east of Brandon. It is a good two lane road with 30, 35, and 40 mph curves. The westbound descent (toward Forest Dale) begins with about a mile of **10%** grade. The road then stair steps the remaining 4 miles down to Forest Dale with short sections of grade that vary from 6% to 3% or less.

The eastbound descent begins with almost a mile of **8-9%** and then stair steps down just like the other side. There is a 15 mph curve at the bottom.

16 US highway 4 *(between Rutland, VT and the junction with Vermont 100.)*

After leaving the junction of US 4 and Vermont 100 there is a one mile 6% climb going west on US 4. At this point there is a sign stating **"Steep grade next 6 miles."** This descent includes short sections of 6% alternating with sections of 3-4%. There are a couple of short sections of 7% descent as you go through the town of Mendon.

17 Vermont 140 *(between Wallingford and Tinmouth, VT.)*

Immediately after leaving the town of Wallingford, westbound 140 begins to climb for about 2½ miles. Much of the grade is **8 or 9%** with a few short sections of milder grade and a few rolling hills. The road is smooth at the bottom and becomes narrow, rough, and winding near the top. The descent toward Tinmouth begins with about ½ mile of 6-8% grade and 20 mph curves. The road then curves and rolls its way the last mile to Tinmouth.

18 Vermont 315 *(from East Rupert to Rupert, VT.)*

The distance between these two towns is about 6 miles with the top of the hill near the middle. The grade is similar on both sides with most of it in the **5 to 8%** range. The exception to this is the first ½ mile of descent on the west side, which is about **12%** grade.

19 Vermont 155 *(between East Wallingford and the junction with highway 100.)*

The top of this hill is about 1½ miles north of the junction. The descent from the top toward East Wallingford begins with a sign stating **"steep grade next 1½ miles."** The grade is **7 to 8%** for about a mile and then the road begins to stair step down with short sections of 5 and 6% alternating with sections of mild or level grade. This continues all the way to East Wallingford, which is about 7 miles from the top of the hill. This is a smooth two lane road.

The descent from the top toward the junction with 100 starts with about ½ mile of 6% and then about a mile of **7 to 8%** grade. There are 35 and 40 mph curves.

20 Vermont highway 100 *(south of Ludlow, VT.)*

Vermont 100 climbs gradually as you make your way out of town. It is a narrow, winding and rough road. About 1½ miles south of town the grade increases to about 5% and quickly thereafter to 9 or 10% for about ½ mile. It eases for ¾ mile and then climbs again for almost 1½ miles at about 8%, which brings you to the top of the hill. As you start the southbound descent there is a sign stating **"10% grade next two miles."** The grade eases to about 6% for the last ½ mile, which brings you to the stop sign at the junction with highway 155.

From this point to the junction with highway 30, highway 100 is almost continuous rolling hills. Some are 6 to 8% but they are never very long.

21   Vermont highway 35 *(between Townshend and Chester, VT.)*

This road is narrow and very rough in many places. There is a one mile section of gravel a few miles south of Cambridgeport. There are rolling hills and short sections of grade that varies from 5 to 7%. The longest continuous grade is about **2 miles of 6 to 7%** that includes the stretch of gravel. This is a descent for northbound traffic. There are also a couple of 10% sections between Grafton and Chester. These are only about ¼ mile long. One is a climb out of Grafton and the other is a climb out of Chester.

22   Vermont 30 *(at Jamaica, VT.)*

As you enter Jamaica from the north on highway 30, there is a **2 mile 8-9%** descent. Highway 30 north of this point is mostly rolling hills.

23   Vermont 100 *(between West Wardsboro and West Dover, VT.)*

This section of highway 100 includes a hill that is **7-9%** for about a mile on both sides.

24   East Dover Road *(between West Dover and Williamsville, VT.)*

Caution! There is a one lane covered bridge just west of Williamsville that has low clearance. When entering the bridge from the west the sign says clearance height is 11'2". When entering from the east the sign says 9'6" clearance. There may or may not be a way around this bridge. Local inquiry should be made if you want to travel this road.

There are two ways to leave West Dover to travel this road. The north fork has a short but very steep climb for a mile or so to where the south fork joins the road. The south fork is a better choice because the grade is minimal. After leaving the point where the forks join, the eastbound climb is about 10% for ½ mile and then 6% for about 1 mile. At this point the descent toward East Dover and Williamsville begins. It is mostly **10% grade for about 3 miles.** It is two lane road with sharp curves. The last 4 miles into Williamsville are mild or flat grade.

25   Vermont highway 9 *(east of Bennington, VT.)*

Six miles east of Bennington there are several warnings for westbound traffic; **"Three miles of steep grade ahead,"** and **"Trucks use lowest gear,"** and **"Trucks 5 mph,"** and flashing yellow warning lights. The descent is **6 to 7%** for most of the **three miles.** There are several signs about the location of the **runaway truck ramp,** which is almost two miles down the grade. It exits to the right and goes uphill. The grade continues at about 7% for almost ½ mile past the escape ramp and then eases to 3 or 4% for the remainder of the drive into Bennington. This section of highway 9 has a third lane for slower vehicles during the long climbs.

About 8 miles west of Wilmington (at Searsburg) there is a steep descent for eastbound traffic. The signs warn: **"Steep grade next 2 miles,"** and **"Runaway truck ramp ½ mile,"** and **"Next ramp one mile."** Most of this grade is **7 to 8%** with one ½ mile section in the middle that is closer to **10%.** There are 25 mph curves. At the bottom of the hill is a sign warning: **"Narrow bridge 1000 feet." They are not kidding. Approach slowly.**

26 Vermont highways 8 and 100 *(south of Searsburg, VT.)*

Both of these highways are good two lane roads with frequent 30 & 35 mph curves. Starting south from the junction of 8 and 9 highways, one immediately climbs a **10%** hill for 3/10 of a mile and then there are about 2 miles of short but steep rolling hills. At this point there is a steep grade warning sign and a 2 mile descent. The first mile is about **10%** followed by one mile of 4 to 6%. About ½ mile later is the junction with highway 100. The first 1½ miles south of this junction are 6% uphill and the next 1½ miles are 6% downhill. After crossing into Massachusetts the road surface gets smoother and the grades milder.

NEW HAMPSHIRE

(The New Hampshire map is combined with the Vermont map on page 6.)

27 New Hampshire highways 25C and 118 *(between Piermont and Lincoln, NH.)*

Heading east from the junction with highway 10, highway 25C is mostly smooth two lane. It is a winding road and the first few miles are rolling hills. About 6 miles east of the junction there is a ½ mile 8% climb and then a short descent followed by a short climb to the top of the hill. At this point there is a sign stating: **"Steep grade, 9% for 2 miles,"** which is accurate.

Highway 118, also known as the Sawyer Highway, starts out rough and the farther east you go the rougher it gets. It is narrow in places, and very curvy. Few, if any, of the curves are marked but most are in the 30 to 35 mph range. The top of the hill is about 7½ miles east of the junction with highway 25. It is a **3 mile 7%** climb up the west side and a **3 mile 8%** descent down the east side. Just before you reach the junction with highway 112, there is another ½ mile of **8%** descent. From this junction to Lincoln is mostly rolling hills.

28 Kinsman Notch *(on New Hampshire highway 112 between Lincoln and the junction with highway 116 north)*

The top of Kinsman Notch is about 6½ miles west of Interstate 93 at Lincoln. The eastbound descent toward Lincoln begins with about ½ mile of 4 to 5% grade. At this point there is a steep grade symbol and this information: **"12% for 2 miles."** It may be that steep for about the first half mile but after that the grade seems to ease somewhat for the next two miles. The last 4 miles into Lincoln are mild grade or rolling hills. This is a fairly good two lane with a climbing lane on the east side of the hill.

The westbound descent starts with a warning: **"9% grade for 2 miles."** The grade is steady for almost two miles. After the first mile the road narrows and there are 30 mph curves. The west side does not have a climbing lane but has a very wide right shoulder during the steep part of the climb. Between the end of the 2 miles of 9% and the junction where 116 turns north, the grade stair steps down gently.

29 New Hampshire highway 18 *(between Interstate 93 and Franconia, NH.)*

After leaving Interstate 93 and heading north on state highway 18 there is a short uphill climb followed by a **2 mile 10%** descent. It is a curvy two lane road with 25 and 30 mph curves.

30 Franconia Notch *(on Interstate 93 between Franconia and Lincoln, NH.)*

The top of Franconia Notch is very near the junction of highway 18 and I-93. The descent to the north toward Franconia is about 4½ miles of grade that is mostly 4-5%.

The southbound descent is unusual because I-93 southbound becomes one lane for several miles as it goes through the narrow part of the notch. The northbound side has two lanes as usual. The southbound grade is gentle through the notch and only 4-5% in sections thereafter. The grade isn't really over until you reach the Pemigewasset River almost 10 miles down from the top of the notch.

Neither side of this hill is steep enough to be a severe problem during descent but both sides are long, slow climbs for heavy vehicles, especially during hot weather.

31 Kancamagus Pass *(on New Hampshire highway 112 between Lincoln and Conway NH)*

The top of Kancamagus Pass is 12 miles east of Lincoln. The westbound descent toward Lincoln begins with a sign stating: **"9% grade for 3.6 miles."** It is a winding two lane road with 30 and 40 mph curves and one 20 mph hairpin turn. After the first ½ mile of 9% the grade seems to ease somewhat. After the 3.6 miles are completed, the grade eases even more to about 3-4% for another 4 miles. The remaining grade to Lincoln is mild.

The eastbound descent toward Conway begins with a warning sign: **"7% grade next 4 miles."** It is a winding road with 35 mph curves and **the 7% grade is steady and lasts almost 5 miles.** The rest of the trip to Conway is rolling hills and mild grade.

32 Bear Notch Road *(between highway 112 and Bartlett, NH.)*

Bear Notch Road is winding and quite rough over much of its length. The top of the hill is almost 4 miles north of the junction with 112. This climb includes a couple of short sections of 6% grade and sections of milder grade. The descent on the north side of the hill includes about **4 miles of steady 6%** that is very rough and winding. This road is closed and gated during the winter months.

33 Pinkham Notch *(on New Hampshire highway 16 between Glen and Gorham.)*

The top of Pinkham Notch is about 12 miles north of Glen. The southbound descent toward Glen begins with about ½ mile of 3-4% grade. At this point there is a sign stating: **"9% grade next 3 miles."** There is a section in the middle of this grade and again at the end of the 3 miles where the grade is much less than 9%. The next 3½ miles include short sections of grade alternating with sections of almost flat roadway. The top 4 miles include a third lane.

The northbound descent begins with three lane highway and a sign stating: **"8% grade next 1.7 miles."** There are short sections in the middle of this 1.7 miles that are less than 8%. At the end of the 1.7 miles you pass the entrance to the Mt. Washington Auto Road. North of this point the grade is mostly 4-5% or less to Gorham.

34 Mt. Washington Auto Road

The entrance to the Mt. Washington Auto Road is a few miles south of Gorham, NH on highway 16. At the gate one is greeted by the following sign: **"Attention: The Mt. Washington Auto Road is a steep, narrow mountain road without guardrails. If you have a fear of heights you may not appreciate this driving experience. Guided tours are available."**

The tours are in what they call "stages" (GMC vans). **The average grade over the 8 mile road is 12%.** Two thirds of the road is paved. They don't allow any vehicle larger than a regular pickup truck, no campers or RVs. This private toll road opened in 1861. The fee for car and driver is $15.00 (in 1996) and increases with additional passengers. The world's highest straight line wind (231 mph) was recorded at the top of Mt. Washington in 1934.

35 Randolph Hill *(on US highway 2 just west of Gorham, NH.)*

As you approach Gorham from the west you will climb a ½ mile 8% hill and then descend a hill with a **runaway truck ramp** at the bottom. At the top of the hill the steep grade sign says: **"8% next 2 miles."** The truck ramp exits to the right and is almost flat. Immediately after the ramp the road narrows to two lanes and the speed limit drops to 30 mph and you enter town.

36 Hurricane Mountain Road *(between Intervale, Kearsarge, and South Chatham, NH.)*

"Not suitable for large vehicles or RVs. Steep winding road. 20 mph." They are not kidding. On many maps this "road" looks just like other county or township roads. It is more like a paved jeep trail straight over the top of the mountain. It is incredibly rough, and steep, and narrow. The sign at the summit says the eastern side is **17% grade for 1.25 miles** and the western side is **15% for 2 miles.** This route might appear to be a shortcut to or from somewhere. Take the long way.

37 Crawford Notch *(on US highway 302 between Fabyan and Bartlett, NH.)*

There is very little grade on the west side of the notch. The eastern descent begins with a sign stating: **"13% grade next 8/10 mile."** The grade certainly doesn't seem like 13% but more like 8 or 9%. In any case it is very short and the grade after that is mild.

38 Tripoli Road *(between Woodstock, Waterville Valley, and Compton, NH.)*

Many maps show this as a paved road that loops from Woodstock through Waterville Valley and back south to Compton. There is a 5 mile section of rough, narrow, steep gravel road between Woodstock and Waterville Valley. The eastbound climb to the top of the hill over this gravel road is **6 to 10%.** When you reach the top the pavement returns but is narrow and quite rough. The descent toward Waterville Valley is about 3 miles, most of which is **9 to 12%.** Highway 49 from Waterville Valley to Compton is good two lane with little grade.

39 Highway 9

Highway 9 includes many short 5 to 6% grades as it crosses New Hampshire and Vermont. These seldom exceed 1½ miles in length. Some sections of the road are narrow and quite curvy, and some are more modern with wider lanes and long sweeping curves. Just west of Keene, NH there is a section where the grade is **7% for 1 mile** on the west side of the hill and **9% for 1 mile** on the east side. Please consult the Vermont section, # 25, for information on two longer hills on highway 9 in Vermont.

EASTERN
NEW YORK

Higher elevations	reds
Middle elevations	golds
Lower elevations	greens

Pass or grade locations	#
Interstate highways	
US highways	
Toll highways	
State highways	

NEW YORK

1 **New York highway 12** *(north of Utica, New York.)*
The junction of 8 and 12 highways is just a few miles north of Utica. The southbound descent into Utica from this junction begins with almost 2 miles of 5-6% grade followed by grade that varies from 3 to 5% all the way to the junction with I-90. The total length of the hill is just under 4 miles.

The northbound descent from the junction of highways 8 and 12 is less than 2 miles long with the top ½ mile in the 5-6% range and the rest 3-4% grade.

Most of the major roads in the **Adirondack Park** are fairly good two lane highways with rolling hills instead of long, steep grades. There are many grades in the 5-6% range but they are usually less than one mile in length. There are a few scattered 7, 8, and 9% grades. The most notable grades in the Adirondack area are numbers 2, 3 and 4 below:

2 **Highway 30** includes a **1.2 mile 8-9%** southbound descent into Blue Mountain Lake. This section of road includes 25 and 40 mph curves.

3 **Highway 73** includes an eastbound descent into Keene. The last **4½ miles** into Keene include **5-9% grades, the last 2 miles of which are steady 8-9%** grade with 35 mph curves.

4 **Highway 9N** includes **2 miles of steady 10-12%** westbound descent as it approaches the junction with 73 just south of Keene.

5 **Whiteface Mountain** *(on the Veterans Memorial Highway, highway 431, west of Wilmington, NY. Elevation 4868')*
This is a long and steep grade: use caution. Immediately after leaving the junction of highways 431 and 86 in Wilmington, the climb on westbound 431 becomes **8% or more** and does not ease until you reach the summit **8 miles** later. Some sections may be as steep as **10%**. The road is quite rough and in some places quite narrow with few places to pull over. It is two lane all the way to the top with one 15 mph hairpin turn and many 25-30 mph curves. There are no escape ramps on the way down. RVs and motorhomes are allowed to make the climb but they must turn around in a fairly small space at the top of the mountain. If you have the option of going up in a smaller vehicle, it might save a great deal of wear and tear on your drive train and brakes. The view of the mountains and Lake Placid is certainly spectacular and well worth the trip. There is a fee.

6 **New York highway 74** *(west of Ticonderoga, NY.)*
There is a **2 mile 7-8%** descent for eastbound traffic as you approach the junction with 9N/22 at Ticonderoga. The westbound descent is much milder grade for about 1½ miles. Highway 74 is a smooth and wide three lane road on both sides of this hill.

7   **New York highway 8** *(east of Hague, NY.)*

The top of this hill is about five miles west of Hague. The eastbound descent toward Hague begins with a sign warning: **"Steep grade next 4.5 miles."** The upper portion of this grade is about 4% and the lower **3 miles are steady 7 to 8% grade**. The road is two lane and the farther you go down the hill the tighter the curves. They are 45 mph curves near the top and by the time you get near the bottom there are several 20 mph curves and finally a 15 mph curve just before you reach the stop sign at the junction of highways 8 and 9N.

The westbound descent is more modern highway that is wider and includes a climbing lane. The speed limit is mostly 55 mph on the west side. The descent is 3 miles long and includes short sections of 4, 6, and 8% grade. The steeper sections alternate with sections of milder grade.

8   **New York highway 9N** *(south of Sabbath Day Point, NY.)*

This is a curvy two lane highway with almost **2 miles** of steep grade on both sides. Most of the grade is in the **7 to 9%** range but the last ¾ mile or so on the east side is closer to **12%**. This is at the bottom of the hill just before reaching Sabbath Day Point.

9   **Massachusetts/New York highway 2** *(between North Adams, MA and Petersburg, NY. Also known as the Taconic Trail.)*

The summit of this hill is at the New York-Massachusetts state line. The descent is **steady 7% for 4 miles on both sides of the hill.** The road is two lane with sharp curves. Some of it is rather narrow. The Massachusetts side is fairly smooth while the New York side is rough. Be advised that there is a stop sign at the bottom of the grade on the Massachusetts side where highway 2 intersects with US highway 7.

There is another summit a little farther west on highway 2 at Grafton, NY. The signs warn of about 4 miles of grade on both sides of this hill but the grade is not as steep or steady on either side as it is on the hill that crosses the state line.

10   **I-88** *(between Schenectady and Binghamton, NY.)*

I-88 has many hills that are several miles long but the grade is usually 4% or less. One exception is near milepost 103 (which is east of Cobleskill) where there is a 2½ mile 6% descent for westbound traffic (climb for eastbound traffic.)

11   **New York highway 28** *(south of Oneonta, NY.)*

About a mile south of I-88, highway 28 begins a **2 mile 6 to 8%** climb. The descent on the south side of the hill is about 2 miles of 6%. It is a rough two lane with 35 mph curves. The road surface improves after the descent on the south side is completed.

12   **New York highway 206** *(from Walton to Downsville and Roscoe, NY.)*

About one mile south of Walton a **2½ mile 10%** climb begins. This is a good two lane road. The descent toward Downsville begins with ½ mile of 6% followed by a short uphill section and then **2½ miles of 7 to 9%** descent.

After going through Downsville there is a climb that lasts almost **5 miles**. The grade varies from **3 to 8%** with most of it about 5%. The descent toward Roscoe begins with almost a **mile of 10%** and then ½ mile of 6 to 7%. There is one more short section of 10% (about 3/10 of a mile) before the descent is over.

13   I-84 *(just east of Port Jervis, NY.)*

The top of this hill is about milepost 4 on I-84 just east of where the borders of New York, New Jersey, and Pennsylvania meet. The eastbound descent is only about 1 mile of 6%. The westbound descent is about **3 miles of steady 6%** followed by 1 mile of 4%.

14   New York highway 17 *(between Monticello and Middletown, NY.)*

A few miles east of Monticello there is a sign that tells eastbound traffic: **"Steep grade next 5 miles."** The descent is about **6% and is quite steady for 4 miles**. At the bottom of the hill there is about a mile of nearly flat road followed by a 5 to 6% climb that lasts almost 2 miles. This climb is followed by another 6% descent that lasts 2 miles and is completed near exit 116.

15   New York highway 52 *(between Ellenville and Walker Valley.)*

The descent from the top of this hill toward Ellenville is almost **4 miles** in length. The top 2½ miles are **7 to 9%** grade followed by a half mile stretch of mild grade. The descent then returns to about 7% the rest of the way into Ellenville.

The descent toward Walker Valley is almost **3 miles** of **steady** grade. The first mile is **6%** and the last 2 miles increase to **7 to 8%**.   This is a fairly good two lane road with 25 and 30 mph curves.

16   US 44/55 *(east of Kerhonkson, NY.)*

This is a rolling, curving two lane road with short grades that vary from 3 to 9%. The longest sustained grade is on the east side and it's a little over a mile in length. It is 8 to 9% and includes a 5 mph hairpin turn.

17   New York highway 214 *(between Phoenicia and Tannersville, NY.)*

Between Phoenicia and Lanesville this road includes a few short hills and 20 and 25 mph curves. Almost 2 miles north of Lanesville a stair stepping climb begins with short sections of 5 to 7% grade that alternate with sections of mild grade. This climb lasts about 3½ miles. The descent on the north side is similar but is only about 2 miles long. After turning east on 23 there is a short steep climb to Tannersville.

18   Green County highway 16 *(between Tannersville and Veteran, NY.)*

This road shows up on the maps but unless you are the adventurous type or you want to see how bad a paved road can be, we suggest you choose another route. There is a stretch of this road west of Blue Mountain that is incredibly steep, rough and narrow. Two cars can barely pass and it is hundreds of feet to the bottom of the canyon with no shoulder. The grade is probably **15% for much of the 3 miles.**

19   New York highway 23A *(east of Tannersville, NY.)*

About 1½ miles east of Tannersville there is a short 9% descent and then a warning sign stating: **"Steep grade next 4 miles."** The grade is **very steady and steep**. It is mostly **8 to 9%** with only a couple of very short sections where the grade eases. There are many sharp curves from 15 mph to 35 mph. The road is two lane with a third climbing lane in some but not all of the steep sections. **Use caution on this road.**

20   New York highway 23 *(between Cairo and Windham, NY.)*

The top of this hill is about 9 miles west of Cairo. The eastbound descent toward Cairo begins with a warning sign stating: **"Steep grade next 2 miles"** but the grade is actually about **4 miles** long. The first 2 miles are **6%** followed by about ½ mile of 4% and then **5 and 6%** for almost 2 more miles. The road is wide and modern with a climbing lane during the entire 4 miles.

The 4 mile westbound descent toward Windham is much more gradual. Most of it is 3 to 4% with a couple of short sections of 6%.

21   New York highway 296 *(between Windham and Hunter, NY.)*

Starting at the junction of 23 and 296 and going south, there is a 10 mph curve and a one mile **8 to 9%** climb. The grade then climbs in short spurts and then rolls up and down with short **7%** hills. The last mile before reaching the junction with 23A is a **10%** descent with a 15 mph curve just before the stop sign at the junction.

22   New York highway 436 *(between Dansville and Nunda, NY.)*

We have not driven this road but it is said to include steep grade warnings for truckers. The eastbound descent into Dansville averages **5% for 4 miles** and the westbound descent into Nunda averages **6% for 3½ miles**. Some sections may be as steep as **8 or 9%**.

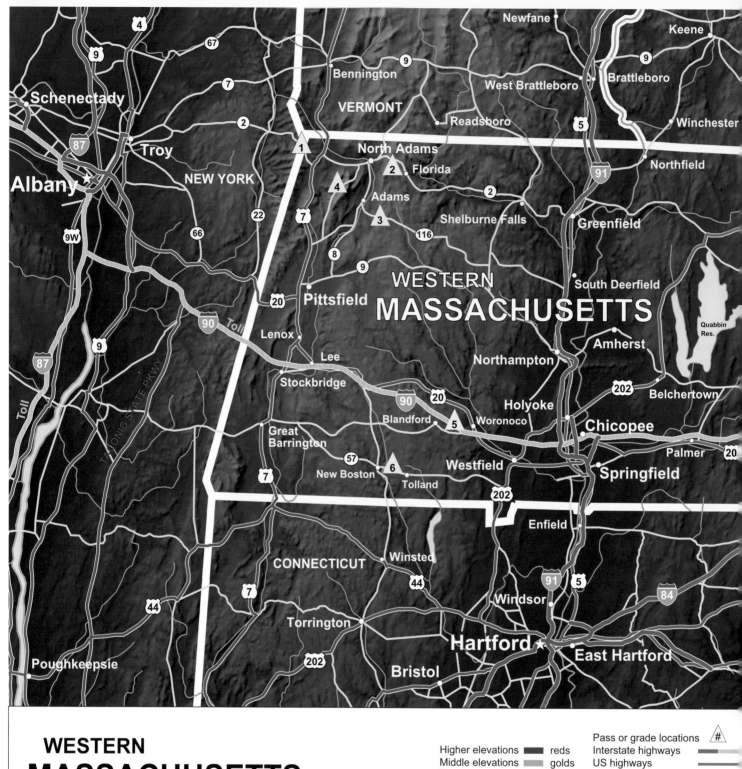

Higher elevations ▬ reds
Middle elevations ▬ golds
Lower elevations ▬ greens

Pass or grade locations ⚠#
Interstate highways ▬
US highways ▬
Toll highways ▬
State highways ▬

1 **Massachusetts/New York highway 2** *(between North Adams, MA. and Petersburg, NY. Also know as the Taconic Trail.)*

The summit of this hill is at the New York-Massachusetts state line. The descent is **steady 7% for 4 miles o both sides of the hill.** The road is two lane with sharp curves. Some of it is rather narrow. The Massachusetts sid is fairly smooth while the New York side is rough. Be advised that there is a stop sign at the bottom of the grade o the Massachusetts side where highway 2 intersects with US highway 7.

There is another summit a little farther west on highway 2 at Grafton, NY. The signs warn of about 4 miles c grade on both sides of this hill but the grade is not as steep or steady on either side as it is on the hill that crosses th state line.

MASSACHUSETTS

2   **Massachusetts highway 2** *(east of North Adams, MA. Also known as Mohawk Trail.)*
The summit of this hill is about 2 miles west of the town of Florida, MA. The eastbound descent begins with about a mile of 6% and then there is a sign over the highway warning: **"Steep hill and sharp curves next 4 miles. Prepare to stop."** The grade is mostly **5 to 6%** with a few short sections of lesser grade. The road is smooth two lane with many curves.

The westbound descent toward North Adams begins with 2½ miles of stair stepping descent with 6 and 7% sections alternating with sections of milder grade. At this point there is a sign over the highway warning: **"Steep grade and sharp curves next 4 miles."** Then there is a sign warning: **"Hairpin turn 4000' ahead."** There are several more warnings about the 15 mph turn as you descend. The grade continues steadily down at about **7% for 4 miles.** The last 1½ miles are in the town of North Adams. **Use caution on this hill.**

3   **Massachusetts highway 116** (east of Adams, MA.)
As you approach Adams from the southeast on 116, the last **5 miles** are a stair-stepping descent with short sections of **5 to 6%** alternating with sections of lesser grade.

4   **Mount Greylock Road** *(near North Adams, MA.)*
Mt. Greylock is the highest point in Massachusetts and there is a paved road over the top. The north end of the road is accessed from highway 2 in North Adams. The south end of the road is on a secondary road between US highway 7 and Massachusetts highway 8. *RVs are not prohibited on this road but.........* From highway 2 in North Adams to the top is almost **9 miles of very narrow, rough, and steep road.** There are sections of **10 to 12%** grade and four or five hairpin turns. Some stretches of road have vertical concrete cylinders lined up on the outside shoulder where the drop-off is quite steep, and there is a ditch and vertical mountainside on the inside shoulder. If two large vehicles meet there is nowhere to go. One RV and one regular size car would have trouble passing in these sections.

The south side of the hill is also about **9 miles of narrow, rough, winding, steep road.** The **10 to 12%** sections don't seem to be as long on the south side. There is an impressive memorial at the top of the mountain and a beautiful stone lodge building. The views are terrific. The trip would be much less stressful in a car or pickup.

5   Interstate 90 (between Woronoco and Blandford, MA.)
This section of I-90 includes a 6-7 mile 4-5% eastbound descent.

WESTERN

PENNSYLVANIA

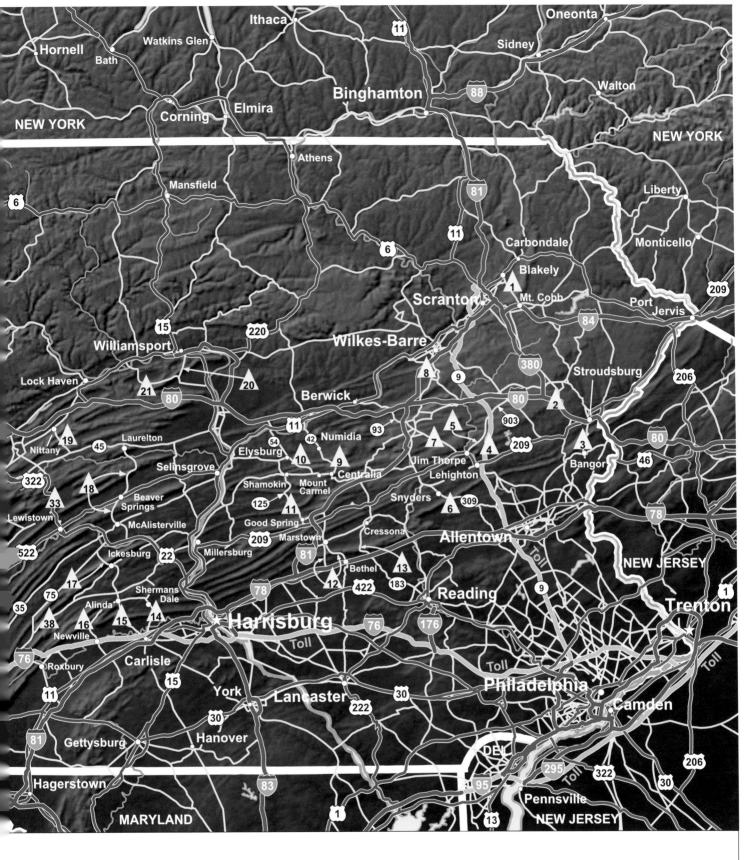

EASTERN

PENNSYLVANIA

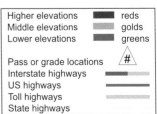

Higher elevations		reds
Middle elevations		golds
Lower elevations		greens
Pass or grade locations		/#\
Interstate highways		
US highways		
Toll highways		
State highways		

PENNSYLVANIA

1 **Pennsylvania highway 247** *(between Mt. Cobb and Blakely, PA.)*

This road is posted: **"Trucks over 10.5 tons prohibited."** About ½ mile after leaving the junction of 247 and I-84, highway 247 climbs one mile at about 6% and then rolls up and down for about a mile. The surface is rough and there are 25 and 35 mph curves. The descent toward Blakely is about **3 miles** of grade that is **steady 8%** except for a ½ mile section of 5% in the middle. There is a **runaway truck ramp** about 2½ miles down from the top of the hill. It exits to the right and is gravel with water barrels at the end. The grade continues past the truck ramp for almost a mile and is still descending as you enter town.

2 **I-80** *(east of the junction with I-380.)*

Just east of the junction of I-380 and I-80, there is a sign for eastbound traffic: **"Steep grade- 4½% next 5 miles."** This eastbound descent is probably not steep enough to pose a problem on the downhill side but does make for a long climb in hot weather for those traveling west on I-80.

3 **Pennsylvania highway 191** *(between Bangor and Stroudsburg, PA.)*

This two lane road is posted: **"Weight limit 15 tons."** The top of this hill is about 5½ miles north of Bangor. The southbound descent toward Bangor begins with a sign stating: **"9% grade next 2¼ miles."** There are a couple of short breaks in the grade during these 2¼ miles and about a mile of 3-4% as you enter Roseto, which is just north of Bangor.

The northbound descent begins with a sign stating: **"13% next 2½ miles."** Much of this hill seems to be more like **10%**. There are 20 mph curves and at the end of the 2½ miles there is a ½ mile **12%** climb followed by a ½ mile **10%** descent, which ends with a stop sign in Stroudsburg.

4 **Pennsylvania Turnpike (highway 9)** *(north of Lehighton, PA.)*

About 12 miles north of the Lehigh Tunnel there is a **steady 5½ mile 4%** descent for southbound traffic. There are more short sections of similar grade all the way past the tunnel. These hills probably won't pose a problem on the downhill side but might make for a long climb in hot weather for northbound traffic.

The tunnel, which is almost a mile long, is posted: **"Clearance 13' 6". Flammable liquids and explosives prohibited."**

5 **Pennsylvania highway 903** *(north of Jim Thorpe, PA.)*

As you approach Jim Thorpe from the north you will encounter a truck pull off area. All trucks over 21,000 pounds are required to stop. In the pull off area there is a map showing the next few miles of road and stating: **"3.3 miles of 8% grade ahead. Sharp curves and residential areas."** Truck speed limit is 20 mph.

The descent is quite **steady** and includes 35 mph curves. Almost 2 miles down from the top you pass the Jim Thorpe Memorial and enter the edge of town. The speed limit is 25 mph. The grade continues through town and includes a 15 mph curve and a stop sign at the bottom just before the junction with highway 209.

6   **Pennsylvania highway 309** *(just east of Snyders, PA.)*

Highway 309 crosses Blue Mountain and the Appalachian Trail just east of Snyders. This is a good two lane highway with climbing lanes during the steep grades. The eastbound descent is about **2½ miles of 7%** grade. The westbound descent is about **2½ miles of 8%** grade.

7   **Pennsylvania highway 93** *(between Jim Thorpe and Nescopeck, PA.)*

Highways 93 and US 209 meet just west of Jim Thorpe, PA. Traveling north from this junction, one immediately begins a **steady 9%** climb that lasts for **2¼ miles**. There is a climbing lane on parts of this hill but not all of it. At the top there is a truck turnout area for southbound traffic where information is available about the grade and the gravel **runaway truck ramp** at the bottom of the hill. The truck speed limit on the descent is 30 mph and there is a stop sign at the junction at the bottom of the hill.

The northbound descent begins with rolling hills for about 1½ miles. At this point there is a sign stating: **"Steep grade - 10% next 2 miles."** The top part of this grade is only about 7% with 45 mph curves. The 10% grade is during the last mile and it is not steady. A few miles farther north there is a hill that is 9% for ¾ mile on both sides and the north side ends in Beaver Meadows.

At the junction of I-81 and highway 93 there is a warning sign for traffic that is northbound on 93: **"Steep grade next 2 miles."** The grade is about **8%** for a little less than 2 miles. As you keep traveling north on 93 there are short, steep, rolling hills until you reach the junction with I-80. At this point there is a 1½ mile 8% climb and then a 2 mile descent that varies from 8 to 5%. From this point to Nescopeck there are rolling hills.

8   **Interstate 81** *(south of Wilkes-Barre, PA.)*

There is a **3½ mile 6%** descent for northbound traffic just before reaching Wilkes-Barre.

9   **Pennsylvania highway 42** *(between Numidia and Centralia, PA.)*

There are several short **8 and 9%** hills along this section of road. There will be both climbs and descents regardless of your direction of travel. The longest **9%** hill is about **1½ miles**.

10   **Pennsylvania highway 54** *(between Mount Carmel and Elysburg, PA.)*

Leaving Mount Carmel and traveling northwest on 54 one first climbs about 1½ miles of stair stepping 7 to 9% grade. After cresting the hill the **2 mile** descent begins with grades that vary from **6 to 9%** followed by a series of short rolling hills and then a **one mile 9%** descent into Elysburg. This is good two lane highway with climbing lanes during the steep grades. The truck speed limit while descending the grades is 20 mph.

11   **Pennsylvania highway 125** *(between Shamokin and Good Spring, PA.)*

Large vehicles may want to avoid this 18 mile section of road. It crosses four mountains and includes numerous 15 mph hairpin turns and many more 20 and 25 mph curves. Regardless of your direction of travel you will have to climb and descend some very steep hills. Much of the grade is **7 to 9%** but there are numerous sections that must be **12% or more**, some lasting almost a mile. Brake shoes don't have enough time to cool much between descents.

12 Pennsylvania highway 501 *(between Marstown and Bethel, PA. ALSO: highway 645 just west of 501.)*

The north side of this hill is posted at **8% for 3½ miles**. It is a **steady** grade but doesn't last quite that long. The south side is posted at **9% for 2¼ miles**. It too is **steady** except for a 1/4 mile section of 7% in the middle and it does last 2¼ miles. This is a two lane road with 40 mph curves.

Highway 645 is **very steep**. The south side is posted at **14% for 1½ miles** and includes a 10 mph curve. The north side is posted at **11% for 1 mile** with 25 mph curves.

13 Highway 183 *(between I-78 and Cressona, PA.)*

The top of this hill is about 3 miles north of the junction with I-78. The south side is posted at **9% for 3½ miles** but the grade is not quite that long and is that steep for only about a mile in the middle with both ends being closer to 6%.

The north side of the hill is posted at **9% for 2¾ miles** and does last that long and includes a ½ mile section of milder grade in the middle of the descent. This road is four lane as you go over the top of the hill and three lane during the climbs. The bottom of this hill is at the junction with highway 895. From this point to Cressona, there are rolling hills that range from 6%-9% and are 1 mile or less in length.

14 Pennsylvania highway 34 *(between Carlisle Springs and Shermans Dale, PA.)*

The grade on both sides of this hill is about **one mile of 8%**. One should use caution when cresting the hill because two other roads intersect with 34 at the summit. The intersection looks like an x with highway 34 being the left half (if you are facing north) and the other roads being the right half.

15 Pennsylvania highway 74 *(between Alinda and Carlisle, PA.)*

The top of this hill, called Waggoners Gap, is about 6 miles south of Alinda. The north side is posted at **8% for 2¼ miles** and it is a **steady** grade with a 10 mph hairpin turn and numerous curves from 20 mph to 40 mph. There is a series of 30 mph curves at the bottom after the grade has ended.

The south side is posted at **8% for 2½ miles** and is also a constant grade. This side is also very curvy and includes two 15 mph hairpin turns. The truck speed limit on both sides is 20 mph.

16 Pennsylvania highway 233 *(between Newville and Alinda, PA.)*

The top of this hill is about 7 miles west of Alinda. The north side of the hill is posted at **7% for 2 miles.** There are few curves during this descent.

The south side of the hill is much more winding and includes a 15 mph curve. The grade is posted at **8% for 2 miles**. With the exception of a couple of miles on the south slope, most of this two lane road is rough.

17 **Pennsylvania highway 74** *(north of Ickesburg, PA.)*

This is a good two lane highway. The south side is posted at **8% for 2 miles**. It is a **steady** grade and some sections seem more like **9 to 10%**. The last ¾ mile at the bottom of the hill is about 5% which makes the whole descent about 3 miles long. There are 20 and 30 mph curves and one 15 mph hairpin turn.

The north side of the hill is not posted but is also **3 miles** long with the top half about **9 to 10%** and the bottom half about **7 to 8%**. There is a 10 mph hairpin turn near the top, 20 and 30 mph curves in the middle and a 10 mph turn at the bottom.

18 **Pennsylvania highway 235** *(between McAlisterville and Laurelton Center.)*

There are two summits on this section of road. The first is between McAlisterville and Beaver Springs. The south side of this hill is about one mile of **9 to 10%** at the top and a very short section of 5 to 6% at the bottom. There are rolling hills along the summit. The north side is posted at **6% for 3 miles** but the middle part seems more like **8%**. This is a good two lane highway with 35 mph curves on both sides of the hill.

The second summit is about 8 miles north of Beaver Springs. The grade on the south side of the hill is not steady. It varies from **5 to 9%** with short sections of nearly flat grade between the steep sections. It is a good two lane road with 30 mph curves.

The grade on the north side is about **2½ miles** long with the top half about **6 to 7%** and the bottom half about **10%**. There are curves ranging from 20 to 35 mph and one 15 mph hairpin turn.

19 **Pennsylvania highway 445** *(between Madisonburg and Nittany, PA.)*

This is a winding back country road with no center stripe or other pavement markings. There is a 10 mph hairpin turn on each side of the hill and a third one at the summit. The steep grade is only about **1½ miles** long on both sides of the hill and varies from **5 to 9%**. After completing the steep part of the descent on the north side, there are several miles of mild grade and very curvy road as you follow the Roaring Run creek toward Nittany.

20 **Pennsylvania highway 554** *(south of Williamsport, PA.)*

The summit of this hill is about 4½ miles south of the junction of 554 and US 15. The grade on the north side of the hill is about **3 miles of 6 to 7%**. It is two lane and includes 25 and 30 mph curves and one 15 mph hairpin turn.

After one 15 mph hairpin turn near the top, the south side is a fairly straight road with 45 mph speed limit. The grade is **7 to 8% for about 3½ miles**.

21 **Pennsylvania highway 44** *(between Elimsport and Collomsville, PA.)*

The Elimsport side of this hill is almost **3 miles of 6 to 7%** grade with 35 mph curves. The Collomsville side is **3 miles** long with the top half about **10%** and the bottom half about **7 to 8%**.

22 **US highway 322/Pennsylvania 153** *(west of Clearfield, PA.)*

These highways split about 5 miles west of Clearfield. There is a **3½ mile 7%** descent as you head toward Clearfield from the split. It is a **very steady** grade. Trucks must stop at the top for information about the grade. It is a divided four lane highway.

23 **Pennsylvania highway 153 and US highway 219** *(between I-80 and Ridgeway, PA.)*

About 5 miles north of I-80 there is a steep grade warning on highway 153 and **trucks over 21,000 lbs must stop** for grade information. The grade is almost **3 miles** long. The first ¾ mile is about 6% followed by a mile of **8 to 10%**. The grade then eases to 4 to 5% for another mile until you reach the stoplight at the junction with highway 255. The highway is three lane during the steep section and the truck speed limit is 20 mph. Truck traffic present.

There is another summit about 5 miles north of the junction with 255. The south side of the hill is about **2½ miles of 7 to 8%** grade. Truck speed limit is 20 mph. The north side starts down with a short 7% grade and then 4 to 5% for about a mile and then back to **7% for 1½ miles**. One half mile later is the junction with US highway 219.

There is a summit on 219 just before entering Ridgeway. The south side of this hill is fairly mild grade for a couple of miles and then about a mile of 6% at the bottom. It is three lane. Before beginning the northbound descent into Ridgeway, **trucks over 7,000 lbs must stop** and read the grade information. There is a **runaway truck ramp** at the top of this hill. Then there is a separate lane on the right for trucks. This becomes a completely different descent and takes the truck traffic over highway 120 where there is another **runaway truck ramp**.

Non-truck traffic will stay in the left lane at the top of the hill and descend about **1½ miles of 8%** grade with **two more runaway truck ramps** on the way down. There is a 15 mph turn at the bottom of the hill.

24 **Pennsylvania highway 144** *(south of Snowshoe, PA.)*

About a mile after leaving Snowshoe on southbound 144, there are rolling hills until you cross over I-80. There are a couple of short 7% descents and then a sign stating: **"Steep grade next 3 miles."** The grade is mostly **7 to 8%** with many 35 mph curves. There are a couple of miles a 4% after the 3 miles of steep grade. It is all two lane.

25 **Pennsylvania highway 504** *(from between Unionville and Philipsburg, PA.)*

The top of this hill is 5½ miles west of Unionville. The descent toward Unionville is about 4 miles long and begins with about **3 miles of 8 to 9%** followed by a mile of **5 to 7%**. There are many curves ranging from 20 mph to 35 mph plus two 10 mph hairpin turns. This is a narrow, smooth road on the east side and narrow, rough road on the west side.

The west side of this hill is a roller coaster ride all the way to Philipsburg. There are no sustained grades but many short climbs and descents that range from **5% to 9%**.

26 **US highway 322** *(between Philipsburg and Port Matilda, PA.)*

The westbound descent into Philipsburg is about 2 miles long. There is a truck pullout at the top for grade information. The grade is **6 to 7%** with a **runaway truck ramp** 1½ miles down from the top. The grade continues at 7% for another 3/10 mile right into town. The truck speed limit is 20 mph. This two lane road is wide and smooth.

The eastbound descent into Port Matilda begins about 5 miles west of town. The two lane becomes divided four lane and the grade is **steady 9% for 2 miles**. Short sections of steep grade alternate with sections of mild grade for the next 1½ miles and then the grade goes to about **7% for 1¾ miles**. There is a **runaway truck ramp** near the bottom of the hill. The truck speed limit is 20 mph.

27   Pennsylvania highway 350 *(between Bald Eagle and Philipsburg, PA.)*

The descent into Bald Eagle is about **2 miles of 6 to 7%**. The road is good two lane with 35 mph curves. The truck speed limit is 30 mph.

The descent into Philipsburg is **1¼ miles of 6 to 7%** grade and most of it is in a **residential** area. Truck speed limit is 20 mph. Between these two descents are rolling hills.

28   Pennsylvania highway 453 *(west of Tyrone, PA.)*

The descent toward Tyrone on highway 453 is posted at **12% for 3½ miles**.   The first two miles appear to be more like **9 or 10%** and the last 1½ miles vary from **5% to 7%** with the grade ending in a **residential** area on the edge of Tyrone. The road is rough, winding two lane, with many 25 and 30 mph curves. The truck speed limit is 20 mph.

The western descent toward the junction of 453 and 253 is milder grade with the last 1½ miles about 6%. The road is smoother on this side.

29   Pennsylvania highway 865 *(west of Bellwood, PA.)*

Highway 865 eastbound includes a **2½ mile 8%** descent followed by short steep sections alternating with sections of mild or flat grade. It is a rough and narrow two lane road with 30 mph curves.

30   Pennsylvania highway 36 *(between Altoona and Ashville, PA.)*

The summit of this hill is about 5 miles west of Altoona. The descent toward Altoona begins with a sign stating: **"6% grade next 2½ miles."** Following this grade there is a short flat section and then a short 6 to 7% climb and then the final descent into Altoona. It is about **1½ miles of 7 to 8%** that continues right into the edge of town. This road is three lane during the steep sections and the truck speed limit is 20 mph.

The westbound descent into Ashville is posted at **"8% grade next 2½ miles"** and this grade also continues right into the edge of town. The truck speed limit is 30 mph.

31   US highway 22 (new and old) *(between Cresson and US 220 (also known as I-99) south of Altoona PA.)*

US highway 22 intersects highway 53 about a mile south of Cresson. About three miles east of the junction there is a warning sign for eastbound traffic on highway 22: **"Steep grade--5% next 7 miles."** The descent lasts all the way to highway 220 but it is not steady. There are two sections where the grade eases to about 2 or 3%. This is divided four lane highway.

What is evidently "old highway 22" intersects highway 53 right in Cresson and begins an eastbound climb while still in town.   The climb is almost **2 miles of 6%**. As you continue east over the summit there is a warning sign for the coming descent: **"11% next 2 miles." Trucks are required to stop** and read the grade information and the truck speed limit is 30 mph. The road is four lane until the end of the 11% section where it becomes two lane and the grade eases to about 7% for ½ mile.

32   US highway 322 *(west of State College, PA.)*

There is a summit just west of town on highway 322. The descent toward the junction with US 220 is **2½ miles of 6%** grade and the hill ends just before the junction. The truck speed limit is 30 mph. It is three lane during the steep section.

The descent toward State College begins with ¾ mile of 8% followed by rolling hills for a short distance, including another 8% hill that is almost ½ mile long.

33   US highway 322 *(between State College and Lewistown, PA.)*

About a mile after leaving Potters Mills on eastbound 322, the road becomes four lane and there is a one mile 5% climb. Almost a mile later there is a warning sign stating: **"Steep grade next 3¼ miles."** **Trucks over 21,000 lbs are required to stop** in the pullout and read the grade information. The first **1½ miles of descent is 8 or 9%.** At this point the road makes a 45 mph curve to the left and the entrance to the **runaway truck ramp** is straight ahead. It is gravel with water barrels at the end. After passing the truck ramp the grade eases for about ¼ mile and then resumes at **6% for 1¼ mile** where it becomes two lane again. Truck speed limit on this hill is 20 mph.

34   Pennsylvania highway 305 *(between Belleville and McAlevys Fort, PA.)*

The east side of this hill is **2 miles** long with **7 to 8%** grades and **10%** for the last 3/10 mile at the bottom. There are 25 and 30 mph curves and two 20 mph hairpin turns.

The west side is posted at **7% for 2½ miles.** The upper 1¾ miles are steady 7% followed by short sections of steep grade alternating with short sections of milder grade and then rolling hills. This is a good two lane highway.

35   Pennsylvania highway 26 *(between McAlevys Fort and Pine Grove Mills, PA.)*

The south side of this hill is about **7%** at the top and gets steeper as you descend. The bottom two thirds of it are **8 to 10%** with 35 mph curves and then rolling hills into McAlevys Fort. The truck speed limit is 30 mph on this side.

The north side is posted at **8% for 2 miles.** It is a **steady** grade with 25 mph curves. The grade continues into town until reaching a stop sign at a T intersection. This is the junction with 45 highway in Pine Grove Mills.

36   Pennsylvania highway 829 *(south of the junction with US 22.)*

The north side of this hill is almost **3½ miles** long with most of the grade about **6%**. There are two ½ mile sections where the grade is **8 to 10%**. The highway is good two lane on the north side but from the top of the hill south it is narrow and rough two lane. There is little descent on the south side. If you continue south on 829 there is a hill south of Cassville that is **10% for one mile** on both sides. The south side includes a 20 mph hairpin turn. It is still narrow and rough road.

37 Pennsylvania highway 641 *(between Shade Gap and Roxbury, PA.)*

Highway 641 crosses two mountains between Shade Gap and Roxbury. The town of Spring Run is in the valley between the two mountains.

The top of the west hill is about two miles west of the junction with highway 75 at Spring Run. The Spring Run side is posted at **10% for 2 miles** but the bottom ¾ mile eases to about 6%. There is a 20 mph hairpin turn near the top.

The Shade Gap (west) side of the hill is posted at **10% for 3½ miles** and it is 10% for most of that length. There are two 15 mph hairpin turns. It is a good two lane road and the truck speed limit is 20 mph on both sides.

The east hill is a more complicated tale. As you leave Spring Run going east on 641, there is a sign stating: **"All trucks over 21,000 lbs gross must use Truck 641."** A little over a mile later the two roads split. Regular 641 climbs at **10 to 12% for almost two miles** and then descends at **10% for 1½ miles**. It then climbs at 6% for about ½ mile where there is a stop sign. This is where Truck 641 rejoins regular 641. At this point there is a sign stating: **"7% next 1½ miles" (the last ½ mile is closer to 10%.)** This, of course, is the last part of the descent toward Roxbury. There are 20 mph curves at the bottom.

Truck 641 is a long loop to the north and the grades are not as severe as 641 because they are spread over a longer distance. It is a bumpy, lumpy, up and down, make you seasick type of road. Regular 641 is a fairly good two lane road.

38 Pennsylvania highway 274 *(between New Germantown and highway 75.)*

The top of this hill is 3½ miles east of the junction with 75. The east side of the hill is posted at **8% for 1 mile** but following that, short steep sections alternate with sections of milder grade most of the way to New Germantown. There is a ½ mile section of 9 or 10% about 2½ miles down the hill.

The west side of the hill is posted at **8% for 2 miles** and there are short sections of 8% thereafter. The last mile to the junction with highway 75 is fairly flat. This is a rough and narrow two lane road.

39 Pennsylvania highway 164 *(between Fredericksburg and highway 26.)*

The west side of this hill is posted at **10% for 2 miles** and the descent ends in the town of Fredericksburg. There are 20 mph curves and the truck speed limit is 20 mph.

The east side is posted at **9% for 2½ miles.** It is 9 to 10% for the entire distance except for one ¼ mile section of 7% in the middle. There are 35 mph curves and a stop sign at the bottom of the grade where 164 intersects highway 26. This is a good two lane road.

40 Pennsylvania highway 913 *(between Robertsdale and New Granada, PA.)*

The east side of this hill is posted at **10% for 3 miles**. It is a **very steady** descent the entire distance.

The west side is posted at **12% for 1½ miles.** Well, I'm from Missouri and you'll have to show me. The top mile is about 6% and the last ½ mile into Robertsdale is about 8 to 9%. This is a mediocre two lane road.

PENNSYLVANIA

41   **US highway 30** *(between McConnellsburg and Fort Loudon, PA.)*
The west side of this hill is posted at **7% for 3 miles**. The upper part is winding two lane and the curves vary from 45 mph to 20 mph and many of them are not marked. About a mile down from the top, the road becomes three lane and the grade is quite steady down to the junction with US 522. The truck speed limit is 20 mph.

The east side of the hill is posted at **9% for 3½ miles**. **Trucks are required to stop** and read the grade information at the top. The grade is **steady 9%** the entire length. About 1¾ mile down from the top the road bears to the left and a **runaway truck ramp** exits straight ahead. It is a long gravel ramp. The 9% grade continues for almost two miles after the escape ramp. Truck speed limit is 20 mph. This is a winding two lane with curves that vary from 25 to 45 mph.

42   **Pennsylvania highway 16** *(between McConnellsburg and Cove Gap, PA.)*
The west side of this hill is posted at **10% for 3 miles**. The upper portion of the grade is 10% but it eases somewhat the last mile or so as you enter McConnellsburg. It is a good two lane and the truck speed limit is 20 mph. **Trucks must stop** and read the grade information at the top of the hill.

The east side is posted at **8% for 3¼ miles** and it is a **steady** grade the entire length. It is a winding road with 45 mph curves and a 20 mph curve near the bottom as you enter Cove Gap.

Highway 456 intersects with 16 about two miles down from the summit.

43   **Pennsylvania highway 456** *(south of the junction with highway 16.)*
From the junction with highway 16, highway 456 begins a **2 mile** descent, most of which is **6 to 8%**. It is a fair two lane road with 40 mph speed limit and 35 mph curves.

44   **US highway 522** *(between Needmore and Webster Mills, PA.)*
Just west of Webster Mills a westbound climb begins that is **6 to 8% for almost 2 miles**. The descent on the other side is **1 mile of 5%** followed by **1 mile of 8 to 9%**. As soon as you reach the bottom a **1 mile 10%** climb begins that includes a 20 mph hairpin turn. After reaching the top the descent toward Needmore is only about ½ mile of 8%. This is a good two lane with 20 mph truck speed limit during the steep descents.

45   **US highway 30** *(between I-70 and McConnellsburg, PA.)*
Immediately after turning onto highway 30 from I-70 (going east) a **2 mile** climb begins that varies from **6 to 8%**. After reaching the top, the grade descends at **6% for 1 mile** and then climbs again for **2 miles at about 7%**.

At the top of this second hill there is a warning for eastbound traffic: **"8% next 3½ miles"** and **trucks are required to stop** and read the grade information. The descent is **steady 8%** with 30 mph curves. About 1½ miles down the road curves to the left and a gravel **runaway truck ramp** exits straight ahead. Immediately after this truck ramp, trucks are supposed to stop again. About ½ mile after the first runaway truck ramp there is a second one that is paved and curves up and out of sight around a hill. About ½ mile past the second ramp, the grade eases to about 5%.

There is a third summit before reaching McConnellsburg and it is about **1½ miles of 8%** on both sides.

34

46 **Pennsylvania highway 915** *(between highway 30 and Hopewell, PA.)*

About 2 miles north of the junction with highway 30, there is a **2½ mile 10%** descent that is quite **steady** with curves that range from 25 to 45 mph. It is a narrow two lane road.

A few miles farther north there is a warning sign: **"10% next 1½ miles"** but the grade only lasts about ½ mile. The grade then climbs at 8% for almost a mile and there is another warning sign: **"12% next 1½ miles."** This grade does last as promised.

47 **Pennsylvania highway 869** *(just east of US 220 (also known as I-99) at St. Clairsville, PA.)*

The east side of this hill is posted at **11% for 1 mile** and it includes two 10 mph hairpin turns. There is a stop sign at the bottom of the hill where 869 intersects with 867.

The west side is posted at **12% for 2 miles** but after one mile the grade eases to about 6%.

48 **Pennsylvania highway 164** *(between East Freedom and Portage, PA.)*

There are two summits on this section of 164. The west summit is about 5 miles east of Portage. The descent toward Portage is posted at **8% for 5 miles** but it is not a steady grade. There are places where the grade eases or is almost flat. The longest sustained section of 8% is near the top and lasts for about 1½ miles. This is a rough two lane road with 25 and 35 mph curves. There is a stop sign at the bottom of the hill as you enter Portage.

Going east from the west summit, the grade is posted at **7% for 1½ miles**. After that descent the road rolls up and down for almost 3 miles and brings you to the east summit. The descent toward East Freedom is posted at **12% for 3 miles**. One mile down from the top a second sign says: **"11% for 2 miles."** The grade does not appear to be that steep. It appears to be more like **9%** and there are a couple of short breaks in the grade. It is a winding road with 20 mph curves.

49 **Pennsylvania highway 869** *(between Beaverdale and Weyant, PA.)*

The towns of Beaverdale and Lloydell have grown together along the highway. The summit of this hill is just east of these towns and the westbound descent toward Lloydell is posted at **15% for 1 mile.** At the bottom of the hill there is a very sharp turn as you enter town.

The eastbound descent toward Weyant begins with about 2 miles of rolling hills. At this point there is a sign warning: **"14% next 3½ miles."** The grade is fairly **steady** the first two miles but appears to be more like **9 or 10%** (except for one very short, very sharp drop right at the top). This is a winding road with 20 mph curves and two hairpin turns. After the first two miles of steep grade the road begins to stair step down with short sections of steep grade alternating with sections of mild or flat grade for several miles.

50 **Pennsylvania highway 56** *(between Pleasantville and Winber, PA.)*

The summit of this hill is about 6 miles west of Pleasantville. The east side is posted at **8½% for 4 miles.** It is a **steady** grade with 20 and 35 mph curves. The grade eases about two miles before you reach Pleasantville. Parts of the road are three lane and the truck speed limit is 20 mph.

The west side is rolling hills to Winber.

51   US highway 22 *(between Blairsville and the junction with highway 271.)*

Traveling westbound on this section of US 22 there are two sustained descents. One is just west of the junction with 271 highway and it is posted at **9% for 2 miles**. It is all of 9% and there is one short break in the grade in the middle. It is three lane and the truck speed limit is 35 mph. There is a great deal of truck traffic on this road.

The other long descent is about 10 miles farther west and it is **8% for 3 miles**. It is a fairly **steady** grade and the truck speed limit is 35 mph. Other than these two descents, the rest of US 22 between Blairsville and highway 271 is constant rolling hills.

52   Pennsylvania highway 271 *(between Ligonier and Johnstown, PA.)*

The summit of this hill is midway between Ligonier and Johnstown. It is **10% for 3 miles** on **both sides**. The Ligonier side has a short break in the grade about a third of the way down. About 1½ miles after the end of the 10%, there is another 1½ miles of 6 to 8%. Truck speed limit is 30 mph.

The Johnstown side eases somewhat for the last mile and then, after several miles of rolling hills, there is a **2 mile 7%** descent in town with a stop light at the bottom. The truck speed limit is 20.

53   Pennsylvania highway 271 *(north of Johnstown, PA.)*

As you enter Johnstown from the north on 271, there is a sign that says trucks over 11,000 lbs are required to take the Truck 271 into town and it splits off to the left. It is **2 miles of 7%** descent. The road that goes straight ahead is not marked as 271 but is the only other choice. There are a series of rolling hills that gradually descend toward town and then a **1 mile 14%** descent that finishes the job. Any vehicle can use this truck route and 2 miles of 7% may appeal to you more than 1 mile of 14%.

54   Pennsylvania highway 56 *(into Johnstown from the east.)*

As you pass US highway 219, the westbound descent on highway 56 is posted at **5% for 5½ miles**. The last mile is 4%. It is four lane divided highway.

55   US highway 30 *(between Ligonier and Bedford, PA.)*

There are two major hills along this road and countless short but steep hills. The summit of the western hill is about 7½ miles east of Ligonier. There are numerous warning signs at the top for westbound trucks. **Placarded vehicles are not allowed down the west side. All trucks over 21,000 lbs gross weight must stop** at the top for grade information and a large pullout is provided. All trucks must stop again part way down the hill. There is a gravel **runaway truck ramp** 3 miles down. Truck speed limit is 20 mph. The grade is **8% for 3½ miles** and ends just before you enter the town of Laughlintown, which is about 3 miles east of Ligonier. The road is all two lane with 20 mph curves.

The east side of the hill is **8 to 10% for 2½ miles** and is all two lane. For the next 19 miles there are many hills to climb and descend that are as steep as 10% but seldom more than a mile long.

The second major hill is at the end of that 19 mile roller coaster ride. About 3 miles east of the junction with highway 160 there is a warning sign for eastbound traffic: **"9% next 6 miles."** This is Bald Knob Summit, elevation 2906'. After one mile of 9% descent, **trucks are required to stop** and read the grade information. They are required to stop again about half way down the hill. Truck speed limit is 20 mph. It is a winding two lane road with 20 and 30 mph curves. At the end of this 6 mile grade there are rolling hills and then another warning sign for eastbound traffic: **"8% next 3 miles"** but the grade only last about a mile and then starts rolling up and down again and continues to roll all the way to Bedford.

56 Pennsylvania Turnpike *(between Bedford and Laurelville, PA.)*

After passing through the Allegheny Tunnel going east, there is a **4-5% descent for 5½ miles.**

There is a summit about 9 miles east of Donegal that is **6 miles of 4 to 5%** on the west side and **3 miles of 4 to 5%** on the east side.

A few miles west of Donegal there is a westbound descent that's **5 miles of 4 to 5%.**

57 Pennsylvania highway 130 *(between Lycippus and Stahlstown, PA.)*

This is a narrow two lane with washed out shoulders. The pavement is fairly smooth and the autumn scenery is great but this is not a good road for large vehicles.

The top of this hill is just east of Lycippus. The west side is **2½ miles** of grade that varies from **6 to 10%** with 25 mph curves and a 10 mph turn at the bottom of the hill. The bottom of the hill is about a mile before you reach Lycippus. The 8 miles of road between Lycippus and Greensburg are constant steep but short hills, both up and down, many of them as steep as **10%**.

The west side of the hill is almost **2 miles** of grade that varies from **7 to 10%** with 30 mph curves. There is a stop sign shortly after the bottom of the grade. This is the junction with highway 711 at Stahlstown.

58 Pennsylvania highway 31 *(between Mount Pleasant and Somerset, PA.)*

A few miles east of Mount Pleasant there is a steep grade for westbound traffic. It is **2 miles of 10%** grade with a **runaway truck ramp** half way down. **Trucks are required to stop** and read the grade information at the top of the hill. It is three lane road. Between the bottom of this grade and Mount Pleasant there are short but steep rolling hills.

Also on highway 31, there is a summit about 7 miles east of the junction with highway 711. The west side is **4 miles of 7%.** Truck speed limit is 20 mph. The east side is about **one mile of 8 or 9%** and then the short but steep rolling hills continue all the way to Somerset.

59 Pennsylvania highway 653 *(from Garrett to Normalville, PA.)*

This a rough, curvy, narrow, two lane road. Immediately upon leaving Garrett westbound, there is a **1¼ mile 8%** climb. The next 20 miles are short but steep rolling hills and endless curves. At this point, which is about 5 miles east of Normalville, there is a westbound descent that is almost all **10 to 12% for 4½ miles** followed by a **½ mile 12%** climb to the junction with highway 381 at Normalville.

60 Pennsylvania highway 711 *(from Normalville to Connellsville, PA.)*

Traveling east into Normalville there is a **2 mile 7 to 8%** descent. It is not steady, but steep sections alternate with sections of mild grade.

The westbound descent into Connellsville is much more severe. It is about **4 miles of 10% or more** with 25 mph curves. Much of the grade is within a residential area.

61 US highway 40 *(east of Uniontown, PA.)*

There is a **3 mile 8 to 9%** descent into Uniontown for westbound traffic on US 40. At the top of the hill, **trucks over 10,000 lbs gross weight are required to stop** and read the grade information and they are required to stop again after the **runaway truck ramp**, which is two miles down from the top of the hill. Truck and bus speed limit on this hill is 10 mph. There is 1 mile of grade left after the runaway truck ramp. The grade on this hill is **quite steady**. This is a four lane divided highway with 40 and 45 mph curves.

There is a **1 mile 9%** descent on the east side of the hill. Between there and I-68 it is a roller coaster ride with constant short but steep rolling hills.

62 Pennsylvania highway 160 *(between Berlin and Wellersburg, PA.)*

After leaving Berlin southbound on highway 160, there are numerous short but steep descents and climbs as you travel across several valleys. About 12 miles south of Berlin there is a warning sign stating: **"13% next 1 mile."** This is really the beginning of a long and steep descent all the way to the Maryland state line.

After descending the one mile of 13% grade, there is a ½ mile climb that is posted at 12%. At the top of this hill there is a sign stating: **"9% next 4 miles."** The grade begins and then eases quickly where there is a pullout where **trucks over 21,000 lbs must stop** before descending the hill. Truck speed limit is 20 mph. The grade resumes and is **steady 9% or more**. About two miles down you enter a residential area where there is a sign stating: **"5% next 1 mile"** but the grade is much closer to **9%** than it is to 5%. The grade continues right through town and finally eases about the time you cross the state line. The grade continues at 3 or 4% and there are 20 mph curves still ahead. During the steep part of the descent there are curves from 25 to 45 mph. It is a good two lane highway.

Pennsylvania highway 160 becomes Maryland highway 47 when you cross the state line and the junction with Maryland highway 36 is only a few miles south of the state line.

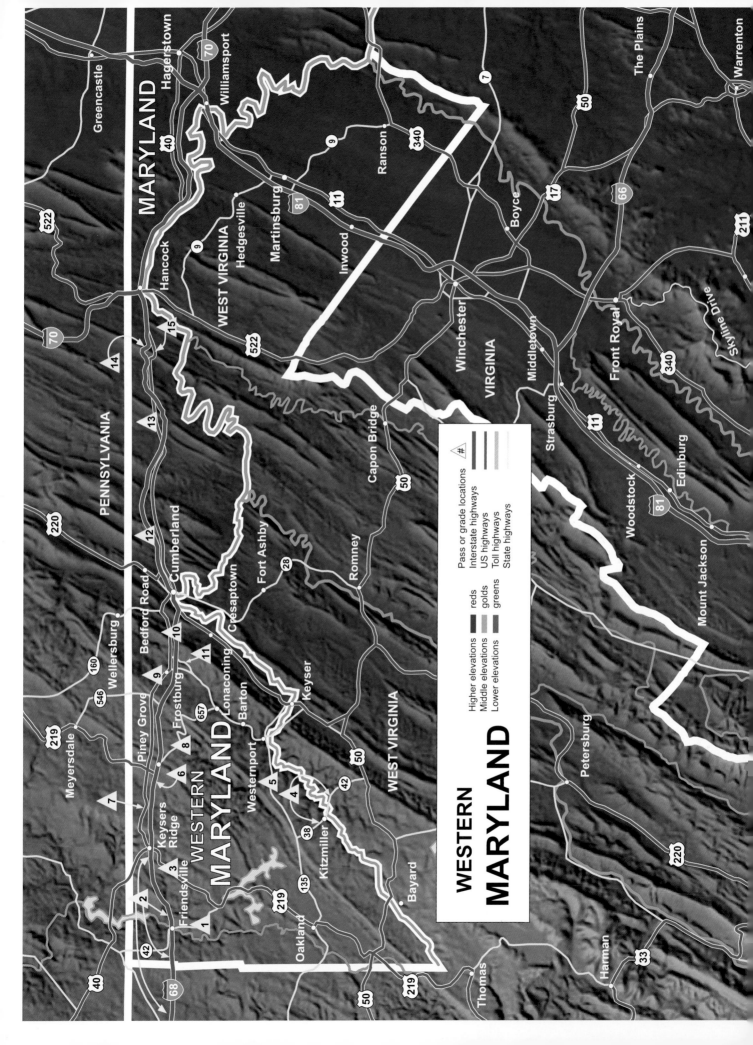

WESTERN
MARYLAND

Pass or grade locations
Interstate highways
US highways
Toll highways
State highways

Higher elevations — reds
Middle elevations — golds
Lower elevations — greens

MARYLAND

1 **Maryland highway 42** *(south of Friendsville, MD.)*

After crossing I-68, southbound 42 climbs for 2 miles. This hill is posted at **8%** and includes many 25 mph curves. Between the top of this hill and the junction with US 219 to the south, highway 42 rolls up and down with short steep hills and many more curves. It is a good two lane road.

2 **I-68** *(between exit 14 (at Keysers Ridge) and Morgantown, WV.)*

There is a fair amount of descent for westbound traffic in the 10 mile section of I-68 between exit 14 and exit 4 at Friendsville, MD. It is not steady the entire length nor is it all steep but it does add up. The first **2 miles** west of exit 14 are about **6%** descent. The next 2½ miles are rolling hills and then, during the last 5 miles to exit 4, the descent varies from **4 to 6%** including a **3 mile stretch of 6%**.

There are several other summits between exit 4 and Morgantown. One is near the Maryland-West Virginia state line. It is **2 miles of 6%** descent on the east side and **1½ miles of 5%** on the west side. There is another summit about 17 miles west of the state line. It is **2½ miles of 5%** on the east side and includes a **runaway truck ramp.** The west side is **4 miles of 5%** that also includes a **runaway truck ramp.** From this point to Morgantown, I-68 is rolling hills.

3 **US highway 219** *(south of I-68.)*

About 1½ miles south of I-68, US 219 descends at **7% for 3 miles.** There is one break in an otherwise **very steady grade.** It is a good three lane road.

4 **West Virginia highway 42 and Maryland highway 38** *(between US highway 50 and Maryland highway 135.)*

About 5 miles north of US 50 there is a **2 mile 8 to 9%** descent on highway 42 that ends when you cross the Potomac River at Kitzmiller. West Virginia highway 42 becomes Maryland highway 38 after crossing the river.

When you enter Kitzmiller from the north, the grade starts all the way back at the junction with highway 135. At this point the warning sign says: **"Steep grade next 5 miles."** One mile down another sign says: **"8% next 4 miles"** and one mile farther down another sign says: **"9% next 3 miles."** The **last two miles of the grade are posted at 11%** and you enter Kitzmiller before it flattens out. **Use caution on this road.**

5 **Maryland highway 135** *(west of Westernport, MD.)*

The summit of Backbone Mountain (elev. 2969') is about ½ mile west of the junction of highways 135 and 38. The descent on the west side is fairly mild. Most of the grade is 4 to 5% with a few short sections of 6%. The last ½ mile before reaching the junction with highway 495 is about 8%.

The eastbound descent is quite different. There is little grade for the first 6 or 7 miles and it is a good 55 mph road. At this point warning signs tell you that there is **"steep grade next 4 miles."** Trucks must stop at the top and they are instructed to ditch the truck immediately if brakes fail. Truck speed limit is 10 mph. Trucks are required to stop again about half way down the hill.

The 4 mile grade is 9% and there is a school zone and a 10 mph right turn at the bottom of the hill. Use caution on this road.

6   I-68 *(at exit 22.)*

There is a **2 mile 6%** descent going west from exit 22 (which is where US highway 219 goes north). There are several shorter 6% climbs and descents to the west.

7   US Alt 40 *(between Keyser's Ridge, MD and US highway 219.)*

Grantsville, MD lies in a valley between Keyser's Ridge and 219. There is a **2 mile 8%** descent into the valley from either side. There are other short but steep climbs and descents along this road. It is a good two lane road.

8   Maryland highway 657 *(between Lonaconing and Piney Grove, MD.)*

This road is not a good choice for large vehicles. It is a roller coaster ride of grades that vary from **6 to 10%**. It is a 12 mile mile trip and only the 2 miles south of Piney Grove are reasonably good two lane. The other 10 miles are extremely narrow and winding and as you descend into Lanaconing the road narrows to barely more than one lane. This is during a 10% grade and there is vertical hill on one side and guardrail on the other. If two large vehicles meet on this section, one must back up or down the hill.

9   US Alt 40 *(eastbound through Frostburg, MD.)*

The summit of Big Savage Mountain (elev. 2900') is about 2 miles west of Frostburg. Eastbound traffic is notified at the top of the hill that there are **9 miles of steep and dangerous road ahead.** It is a heavily congested area, including through downtown Frostburg. **Truckers are instructed to descend in lower gear and if brakes fail to ditch the truck immediately. Trucks are required to stop at the top and again in the middle of the hill. Trucks over 10,000 lbs are not allowed on this hill.**

The upper part of the grade is about **10%**. This continues right into town where there is a stop light at the junction with highway 36. The grade continues at about **7%** for another **4 or 5 miles** with sections of steep grade alternating with sections of mild or flat grade. **Use caution on this road.**

Going west on Alt 40 from the top of Big Savage Mountain, the road rolls up and down with short but steep hills to the junction with US highway 219.

10   I-68 *(west of Cumberland, MD.)*

At milepost 30 (which is approximately where highway 546 intersects I-68, just west of Frostburg) there is a warning for eastbound traffic: "6% next 13 miles." All vehicles over 5 tons gross weight must exit at weigh station. The truck speed limit is 45 mph. There are several breaks in the grade during this descent but they are not long enough to allow complete cooling of brakes. There have been many accidents on this hill due to brake fade. The last few miles of the descent are in the congested area of Cumberland and there are 40 mph curves to negotiate. There are no escape ramps but one can pull off onto the shoulder to let brakes cool.

11 Maryland highway 55 *(south of Frostburg, MD.)*

Highway 55 descends all the way from the junction with highway 36 to the junction with US Alt 40. It is mostly **6 to 8% for 2½ miles**. It is a good two lane road.

12 I-68 *(at exit 52.)*

There is a summit at exit 52 which is posted at **6% for 2½ miles** on the east side and 6% **for 3 miles** on the west side.

13 US 40 Scenic *(between I-68 exits 62 and 68.)*

This road is a roller coaster ride consisting of short **8 to 10%** climbs and descents with sharp curves. It is rather narrow for large vehicles.

14 I-68 *(at milepost 74.)*

There is a summit near milepost 74 and the east side is about **3 miles of 6%** with a **runaway truck ramp** almost half way down. The west side is about **2 miles of 6%** with a **runaway truck ramp** near the bottom.

15 US 40 Scenic *(east of exit 75 on I-68.)*

This section of US 40 is good three lane road. The west side of the hill is about **2 miles of 7%** and the east side is about **3 miles of 7%**. The grade is **quite steady on both sides.** If you are eastbound, US 40 will turn into highway 144 and it is a series of short steep hills and sharp curves to Hancock.

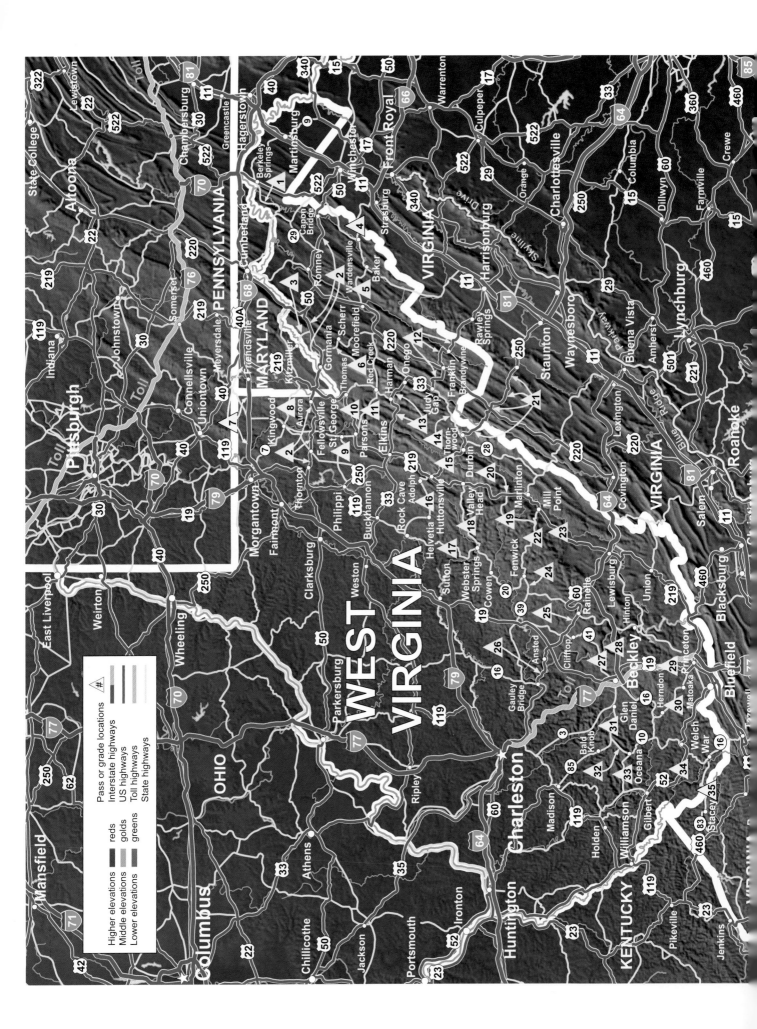

WEST VIRGINIA

1   **West Virginia highway 9** *(between Berkeley Springs and highway 29.)*
Much of this road includes short but steep climbs and descents. Some are as steep as **8 or 9%** but they rarely exceed **1½ miles** in length. One exception is a hill just east of the junction with highway 29. It is **one mile of 7%** climb from the junction to the top and then about **3 miles of 6 to 9%** descent. After you cross the river at the bottom the rolling hills begin.

It's about 20 miles across this road and, with the exception of an 8 mile section in the middle, it is continuous hills and sharp curves.

2   **US 50** *(between Thornton and Capon Bridge, WV.)*
There is hardly a flat or straight section of road between these two towns. There is a minor summit about 1½ mile east of Thornton. It is **7 to 9% on both sides**. The west side is 1½ miles long and ends in Thornton. The east side is about 1 mile long. There are numerous 20 to 35 mph curves on both sides. Two lane road.

There is another summit east of Fellowsville, WV. The west side is **4½ miles of 6 to 7%** with many 30 to 40 mph curves. The east side is **3 miles of 7 to 9%** (mostly 9%) with many curves, including three 15 mph hairpin turns.

The town of Aurora is near the top of Cheat Mountain. The west side of this hill is posted at **9% for 3 miles. All trucks must stop and check brakes.** The descent is **steady** grade with constant 20 to 35 mph curves. The descent on the east side begins near Aurora and is more gradual, descending in 4 to 5% sections alternating with sections of mild or flat grade. Between this point and the junction of US 50 and 42 North, there are many climbs and descents, most of them **6 to 9%**, and most of them less than two miles in length. There is a **2 mile 9%** descent into Gormania for westbound traffic.

At the junction with 42 North there is a warning sign for eastbound traffic on US 50: **"9% next 5 miles."** This is a **very steady** grade for the entire 5 miles and it includes many sharp curves. There are two 15 mph hairpin turns. It is all two lane. The grade eases about 2½ miles before you reach the junction with US 220. **Use caution on this road.**

US 220 South and US 50 East converge and become one road for about 12 miles. There is one hill toward the west end of this section that is **1 mile of 9%** on each side. The rest of the road is rolling hills or mild grade but almost constant sharp curves until highway 220 splits and turns south. The road opens up somewhat from there to Romney. Between Romney and Capon Bridge, there are several short but steep climbs and descents, some as steep as 9%. The longest steep section is at a summit about 5 miles west of Capon Bridge where the grade is **7% for 2 miles on both sides** of the hill. There are sharp curves and the road is two lane with occasional climbing lanes.

45

3   **West Virginia highway 42 and Maryland highway 38** *(between US highway 50 and Maryland highway 135.)*

About 5 miles north of US 50 there is a **2 mile 8 to 9%** descent on highway 42 that ends when you cross the Potomac River at Kitzmiller. West Virginia highway 42 becomes Maryland highway 38 after crossing the river.

When you enter Kitzmiller from the north, the grade starts all the way back at the junction with highway 135. At this point the warning sign says: **"Steep grade next 5 miles."** One mile down another sign says: **"8% next 4 miles"** and one mile farther down another sign says: **"9% next 3 miles."** The last **two miles** of the grade are posted at **11%** and you enter Kitzmiller before it flattens out. **Use caution on this road.**

4   **Virginia highway 55** *(between I-81 and Wardensville, WV.)*

The summit of this hill is at the Virginia-West Virginia state line. The east side is about **4½ miles** of grade that is about **6%** during the top mile, then eases to 2 or 3% for a mile and then varies from **5% to 9%** during the last two miles, getting steeper as you descend. Between the bottom of this grade and I-81, there are rolling hills, some of which are as much as 9% but not as long.

The west side of the hill is posted at **9% for 4 miles**. The upper two miles are steady 9% but the last two miles ease somewhat to about 7%. This is a good two lane road with curves that range from 30 to 40 mph during the steep sections.

5   **West Virginia highway 55** *(between Baker and Moorefield, WV.)*

There are 4 summits along this stretch of highway 55. The longest grade is the last descent toward Moorefield, which is 3 miles long and includes a 15 mph hairpin turn. It is **9% for the first two miles and then 1 mile of 8%.** The other climbs and descents back toward Baker are usually in the 9% range but all are two miles or less in length. This is all two lane road with many curves from 25 mph to 45 mph.

6   **West Virginia highway 42** *(between Mount Storm and Scherr, WV.)*

The top of this hill is 4 miles north of Scherr. The southbound descent toward Scherr is posted at **10% for 4 miles**. It is a **steady** grade with almost continuous 25 and 30 mph curves. The northbound descent toward Mount Storm is more gradual and includes rolling hills.

This is all two lane road with coal truck traffic. South of Scherr the road is narrow and rough.

7   **I-68** *(between exit 14 (junction with US 219 south in Maryland) and Morgantown, WV.)*

There is a fair amount of descent for westbound traffic in the 10 mile section of I-68 between exit 14 and exit 4 at Friendsville, MD. It is not steady the entire length nor is it all steep but it does add up. The first 2 miles west of exit 14 are about **6%** descent. The next 2½ miles are rolling hills and then the last **5 miles** to exit 4, the descent varies from **4 to 6%** including one **3 mile stretch of 6%.**

There are several other summits between exit 4 and Morgantown. One is near the Maryland-West Virginia state line. It is **2 miles of 6%** descent on the east side and **1½ miles of 5%** on the west side. Another summit is about 17 miles west of the state line. It is 2½ miles of 5% on the east side and includes a runaway truck ramp. The west side is 4 miles of 5% that also includes a runaway truck ramp. From this point to Morgantown, I-68 is rolling hills.

8   **West Virginia highway 7** *(east of Kingwood, WV.)*

The top of this hill is 5 miles east of Kingwood. The westbound descent toward Kingwood is posted at **9% for 3 miles**. This is a **steady** grade with 30 and 40 mph curves. It is two lane road. **Trucks are required to stop** at a pulloff, which is ½ mile down from the top of the hill. There is a gravel **runaway truck ramp** almost 2 miles down from the top. There is little descent on the east side.

9   **West Virginia highway 38** *(between Philippi and St. George, WV.)*

This two lane road includes several climbs and descents, the longest of which is a **2 mile 9%** descent for westbound traffic. Curves range from 20 to 45 mph.

10   **US 219** *(between Thomas and Parsons, WV.)*

There are many coal and logging trucks on this road. The top of this hill is about 6 miles south of Thomas. The northbound descent toward Thomas is rolling hills. The southbound descent is posted at **6% for 5½ miles**. Much of the grade may be steeper than 6%.

The first 2½ miles are **very steady** grade with 35 and 40 mph curves. At this point there is a very short flat spot where **trucks are required to stop** and check brakes. There are still **3 miles of 6%** remaining. About ½ mile after the truck turnout there is a 20 mph hairpin turn and then more 35 and 45 mph curves. The grade bottoms out at the junction where highway 72 turns south.

By the way, most maps show a paved road that parallels this section of US 219. It goes through Lead Mine. If you think it might be a better choice, the sign that greets you as you turn onto it from US 219 says: **"10% next 5 miles."** It is paved but only **one lane wide.**

11   **West Virginia highway 72** *(between Parsons and Red Creek, WV.)*

This road is posted: **"Closed to through truck traffic"** and **"Narrow road and sharp curves next 15 miles."** This road is so narrow there is no center stripe. There are places where there is a guardrail on one side and vertical rocks on the other and two large vehicles could not pass. Many places there is no guardrail and the shoulder is extremely narrow before a long drop-off down the side of the mountain. The climbs and descents are seldom over a mile long but they are very steep, usually **10 to 12%.** The road is narrow and winding and includes six hairpin turns.

12   US 33 *(between Harrisonburg, VA and Judy Gap, WV.)*

There are three summits along this stretch of US 33. The eastern summit is between Rawley Springs, VA and Brandywine, WV. The east side is **4 miles of 8 to 9%** grade. The west side is **4½ miles of 9%** grade and both sides have continuous sharp curves and hairpin turns. The highway is two lane on both sides.

The middle summit is between Oak Flat and Franklin, WV. The east side of this hill is **2½ miles of 8%** with 25 mph curves. The west side is about 3½ miles of much milder grade. It is **4 to 5%** over most of its length. There are some sharp curves near the bottom. The road is two lane on both sides of the hill.

The western summit is between Franklin and Judy Gap, WV. It is **5 miles of steady 9%** grade on **both sides**. Both sides are two lane with sharp curves and hairpin turns. **Use caution on this road**.

13   US 33 *(between Onego and Elkins, WV.)*

There is a summit about midway between Onego and Harman, WV. The west side is posted at **9% for 2 miles**. The east side is posted at **10% for 3½ miles**. The east side is a **very steady** grade with 25 and 30 mph curves and a climbing lane that comes and goes. The west side is not as steady but there is still plenty of grade with 30 and 40 mph curves.

There are several summits between Harman and Elkins. The climbs and descents are in the **8 to 9%** range and are **2 miles or less** in length with one exception. This is the first summit west of Harman. It is posted at **9% for 3½ miles** on the east side. The road between Harman and Elkins is all good two lane except for the last 9 miles into Elkins, which is divided four lane.

14   West Virginia highway 28 *(between Judy Gap and Thornwood, WV.)*

The top of this hill is about 8 miles north of the junction of 28 and US 250. The north side is about **4½ miles of 6 to 7%** with 40 and 50 mph curves. The south side is rolling hills near the top and then **2 miles of 9%** descent followed by short flat sections alternating with short steep sections for several miles. This is all fairly smooth two lane that is a bit narrow at times.

15   US 250 *(between Durbin and Huttonsville, WV.)*

The summit of this hill is about 8½ miles south of Huttonsville. The descent toward Huttonsville is posted at **9% for 4 miles**. It is a **steady** grade with 30 to 45 mph curves and a 15 mph hairpin turn near the bottom.

Going south from the summit the highway rolls up and down for about 6 miles and then a descent begins that is posted at **8% for 1½ miles**. This is really a 3 mile hill because after the first descent there is a ½ mile flat section and then another descent begins that is posted at **8½% for 1½ miles**. This descent includes 25 to 35 mph curves. Highway 250 is two lane and is narrow in places.

16 **The Adolph-Helvetia Road** *(between Mill Creek and Rock Cave, WV.)*

This is a narrow, rough and winding road that is most often used by local residents and coal trucks. There are a number of climbs and descents that are in the **9 to 10%** range. Several are as long as **2½ miles** but most are shorter. There are two one lane bridges and a number of hairpin turns. **This is not a very good road for large vehicles.**

17 **West Virginia highway 20** *(between Rock Cave and Cowen, WV.)*

This road is almost continuous climbs, descents, and curves, with a few hairpin turns thrown in for good measure. The longer hills are between Hacker Valley and just south of Webster Springs. About 5 miles south of Hacker Valley there is a summit with a **3 mile 7 to 9%** grade on the north side. The south side is **3½ miles of 7 to 9%** followed by **2 miles** of intermittent **5%** descent. Both sides include 25 to 35 mph curves. The south side bottoms out about 9 miles north of Webster Springs.

Webster Springs is in a valley and there is a steep descent from both north and south as you enter town. The descent from the north is **2 miles of 9 to 10%** with 25 to 35 mph curves. The descent from the south is posted at **6% for 2½ miles** but only the top mile is 6%. There are two 15 mph hairpin turns and below the top hairpin the grade goes to about **10%** for the remaining 1½ miles to Webster Springs.

18 **West Virginia highway 15** *(between Webster Springs and Valley Head, WV.)*

This road climbs out of Webster Springs and then rolls up and down along the ridge of the mountains for about 18 miles before beginning the descent toward Valley Head. It is good two lane with occasional rough spots.

The westbound descent toward Webster Springs is about **5½ miles** of grade that varies from **6 to 9%.** There are curves from 20 to 35 mph and one hairpin that is marked at 15 mph.

The eastbound descent toward Valley Head is about **3½ miles** of grade that varies from **5 to 8%** with continuous curves.

19 **West Virginia highway 150** *(also known as "Highland Scenic Highway" west of Marlinton.)*

No trucks are allowed on 150 except by permit.

This road includes some very long and steep grades. It is a good two lane without sharp curves. The speed limit is 45 mph. Going south from US 219 there is a **3 mile 7%** climb. About 3 miles later there is a **3 mile 8%** descent and then a **5 mile** climb, most of which is **7 to 9%.** This brings you to Black Mountain summit (elevation 4545'). From this point the road rolls up and down for almost 7 miles and then there is a **2 mile 8 to 9%** descent to the junction with highway 39/55.

20 **US 219** *(north of Marlinton, WV.)*

The top of this hill is at the junction with highway 150, which is about 6 miles north of Marlinton. The north side of the hill is posted at **8% for 2 miles** and includes 20, 30, and 45 mph curves.

The south side of the hill is posted at **8% for 3½ miles** but after that descent there is a one mile break in the grade and then another **1½ miles of 8%** that takes you right to the edge of town. The grade includes 20 and 25 mph curves. US highway 219 is a bit narrow.

21   **US 250** *(from Thornwood, WV to Staunton, VA.)*
     There are a number of summits along this part of US 250. Starting from Thornwood, West Virginia and going east:

   (1) This summit is at the state line. The west side is **3 miles of 9%** and the east side is **4 miles of 9%**. There are continuous sharp curves and hairpins on both sides.

   (2) This hill is **1 mile of 9%** on the west side and **2 miles of 9%** on the east side. Sharp curves and hairpin turns on both sides. There are rolling hills through the valley before starting up the next grade.

   (3) This hill is **2 miles of 9%** on **both sides**, again with sharp curves and hairpins. On the east side the grade continues right through the town of Monterey, VA.

   (4) This hill is **2 miles of 7 to 8% on both sides** with sharp curves and hairpin turns.

   (5) **Ditto the above.**

   (6) **Ditto the above except only 1 mile on each side.** The east side of this hill bottoms out at the town of Head Waters, VA.

   (7) This hill is **2 miles of 9%** on both sides with sharp curves and hairpin turns. The town of West Augusta is about 5 miles east of the bottom of this hill.

22   **West Virginia highway 39/55** *(west of Mill Point, WV.)*
     The top of this hill is about 9 miles west of Mill Point and the junction with US 219. The west side is posted at **9% for 2 miles**. It is a good two lane with 35 mph curves.

     The east side is posted at **9% for 5 miles**. The upper 3 miles of this descent may be a little less than 9% but the last 2 miles are 9% with sharp curves.

23   **US 219** *(between Lewisburg and Marlinton, WV.)*
     This stretch of US 219 includes many short **8 to 9%** climbs and descents. Two of these hills are about **2½ miles** long. The rest are shorter but almost all have sharp curves.

24   **West Virginia highway 39** *(west of Fenwick, WV.)*
     The eastbound descent into Fenwick is posted at **8% for 2½ miles**. This is a good two lane road (short section of three lane near the top) with 30 to 45 mph curves. There is a stop sign at the bottom of the hill at the junction with highway 20 north.

25   **US 60** *(west of Rainelle, WV.)*
     As you leave Rainelle going west on US 60 there is a sign telling you to expect curves for the next 7 miles. At the same time you start up a **3 mile 8%** grade. The 20 and 25 mph curves are constant. After topping this hill there are 8% climbs and descents for the next 4 miles to accompany the rest of the curves. These hills are 1 mile or less in length. This is a fair two lane with an occasional climbing lane.

26   **US 60** *(between Ansted and Gauley Bridge, WV.)*

There are several **8%** climbs and descents along this section of US 60. The longest is the **2½ mile 8%** descent into Gauley Bridge. The others are 1½ miles or less in length. All of these hills include almost continuous sharp curves (20 to 25 mph) with an occasional 15 mph hairpin turn. This is fairly good two lane with an occasional climbing lane.

27   **West Virginia highway 41** *(between Beckley and Clifftop, WV.)*

Highway 41 descends into the famous New River Gorge northeast of Beckley. This road is smooth but narrow and many of the sharp curves are not marked.

After leaving Beckley, northbound on 41, the road rolls up and down with short but steep hills and lots of curves. When the steady part of the descent finally begins, it is **3 miles of 8 to 9%** with continuous sharp curves and a 15 mph hairpin at the bottom.

The descent into the gorge from Clifftop, going south on 41, is spread over a longer distance (about 7 miles) and there are short sections of **8 to 9%** alternating with longer sections of milder grade. Some of the steeper sections include sharp unmarked curves.

28   **I-64** *(east of Beckley, WV.)*

There is a **5 mile 7%** descent for eastbound traffic on I-64 and it begins near milepost 133 and ends at the New River near Sandstone, WV. This is a **very steady** grade. The speed limit for trucks over 30,000 lbs is 45 mph. There are **two runaway truck ramps**. The first is about 3 miles down from the top of the hill. It slopes down at the same grade as the highway and is very long. The second ramp is one mile after the first and exits to the right and slopes uphill steeply. It also curves to the right as it goes uphill. There is about ¾ of a mile of steep grade left after the second escape ramp. **Use caution on this road.**

Farther east on I-64 there is a descent for westbound traffic. It is roughly between Dawson and Green Sulpher Springs. The top of the hill is near milepost 148 and it is posted at **7% for 4 miles**. There is a **runaway truck ramp** about one mile down from the top of the hill. It exits to the right and slopes uphill and curves to the right. The upper two miles are **steady 7%** but the lower two miles may be a bit less than 7%.

29   **I-77** *(between Beckley and Princeton, WV.)*

About midway between Beckley and Princeton, (near milepost 27) a southbound descent begins from the summit of Flat Top Mountain, elevation 3252'. It is posted as a **5 mile 5%** grade. There are a few short breaks in the grade and a sharp curve at the bottom. There is little descent on the north side.

30   **West Virginia highway 10** *(between Herndon and Matoaka, WV.)*

There are several short but steep climbs and descents along highway 10.   Most are only a mile or so long. The hill between Herndon and Matoaka is longer. It is **3 miles of 7 to 9%** on the west side and **2¼ miles of 7 to 8%** on the east side. Both sides have continuous sharp curves and hairpin turns.

31 West Virginia highway 99 *(between Glen Daniel and highway 85.)*

The summit of this hill is about two miles east of the junction of 99 and 85 highways. The westbound descent is **2 miles of 8 to 9%** until you get to the stop sign at the junction of 85. This is a T intersection where 99 ends and you must go north or south on 85. See next entry (32) for description of highway 85.

The eastbound descent on 99 begins with about **2½ miles of 8 to 9%** and then steep rolling hills and then another **2 mile** section of **8 to 9%** descent followed by **1 mile of 6%**. The overall descent is almost **7 miles** with 25 and 30 mph curves. **Use caution on this hill.**

This is a two lane road that has been cut through solid rock in a very dramatic fashion. It is fairly good road with a few very rough spots. There is coal truck traffic.

32 West Virginia highway 85 *(between Bald Knob and Oceana, WV.)*

The top of this hill is about ½ mile south of the junction of 85 and 99 highways. The northbound descent is **3½ miles of 9%**. It is **very steady** grade with sharp curves near the top and then more open road as you descend.

The southbound descent is **2 miles of 9%** with a sharp curve in the middle of the grade. (If you have come west on 99 and then turn north on 85 you will have a combined descent of about **5 miles of steady 9%.**)

33 West Virginia highway 10 *(between Cyclone and Oceana, WV.)*

This hill is about **2 miles of 7 to 9% on both sides**. Both sides have almost continuous sharp curves and occasional hairpin turns, few of which are marked. The road itself is not too bad but beware of gravel shoulders that are often deep ruts at the edge of the pavement.

34 US 52 *(between Williamson and Bluefield, WV.)*

This tedious road is quite narrow with bad shoulders and endless curves. There are several climbs and descents that last 2 miles or less and have grades that are usually in the **8 to 9%** range. (One is posted at **11% for 1½ miles**. This is a southbound descent and is about 7 miles south of Williamson.) These hills are near Williamson, Gilbert, Welch, and Bluefield. Be very careful of the sharp curves that can present themselves without warning signs.

35 Highway 83 *(at the Virginia-West Virginia state line (between War, WV and Stacy, VA.)*

The east side of this hill is about **2½ miles of 7 to 9%** with continuous sharp curves and hairpin turns. At the summit the road rolls up and down along the ridge for almost two miles. The west side of the hill is also about **2½ miles of 7 to 9%** grade with sharp curves and hairpin turns.

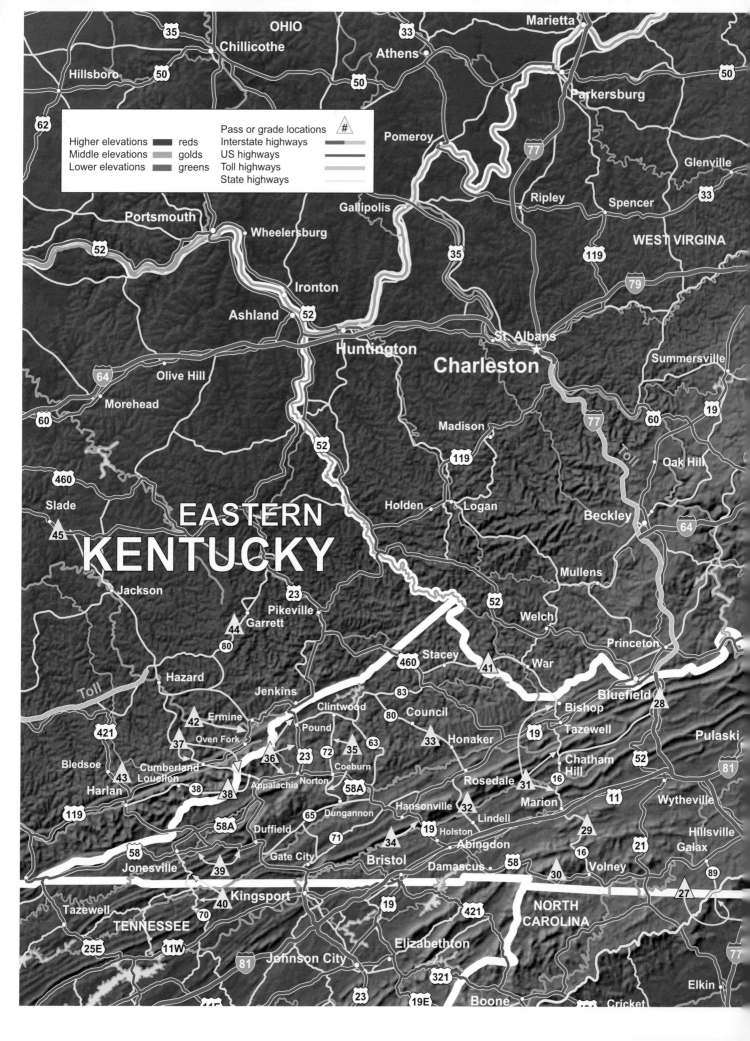

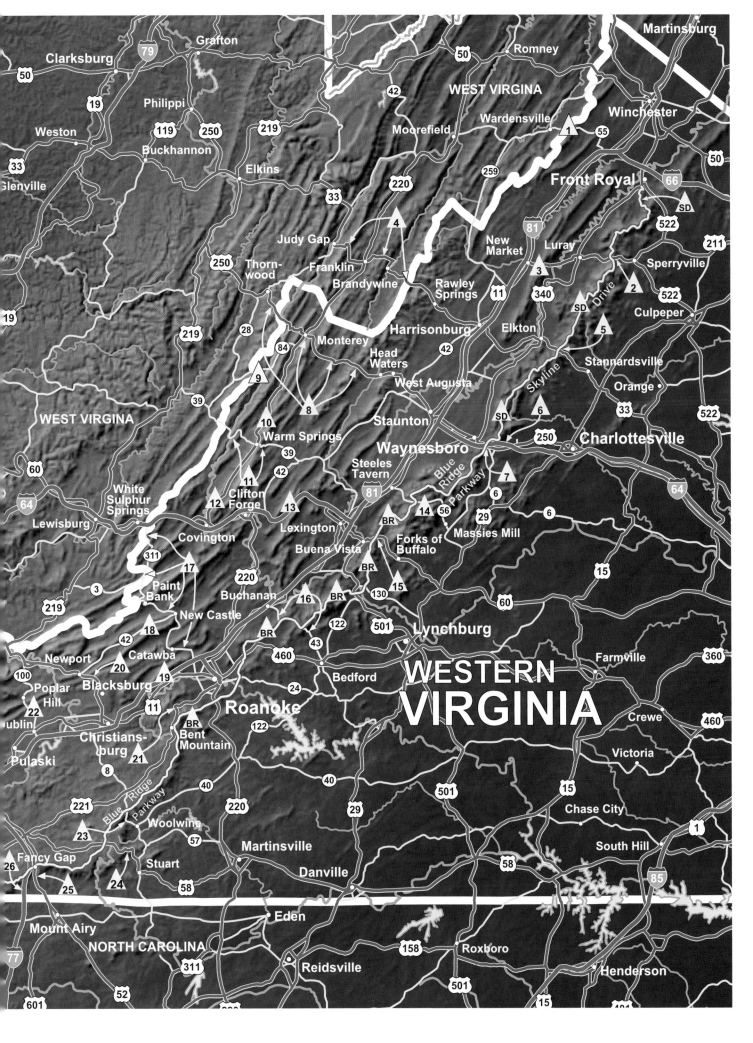

VIRGINIA & KENTUCKY

SD Skyline Drive *(between Front Royal and Waynesboro, VA.)*

This is smooth two lane road with many pullouts for viewing the scenery. The speed limit the entire 105 mile distance is 35 mph and the curves are almost constant. The longest grades are where you get onto Skyline Drive from the major highways that intersect it. At the north end, the steady climb from Front Royal (highway 55/340) to Signal Knob Overlook is about **5½ miles of 6 to 7%**.

The descent to US highway 211 from the north is not too bad because it is spread out over a longer distance and doesn't drop as much. The southbound climb from 211 is about **3½ miles of 6 to 7%** and includes a short arched tunnel with 12' 10" vertical clearance.

The descent to US highway 33 from the north is about **4½ miles of 6%** and the southbound climb from US 33 is 6% but only a mile or two long.

The southbound descent to I-64 is about **3 miles of 4 to 5%**.

Other than the grades mentioned above, the only long, steep grades are between US 211 and the north entrance to Skyline Drive. They are from **2 to 3¼ miles** long and may have sections of **7 to 8%** but will average about **6%**. Of course, there are many short hills all along this road.

BR The Blue Ridge Parkway *(from Waynesboro to Roanoke, VA.)*

When you head south on the Parkway from I-64, you are beginning at an elevation of 1900 feet. The climb to Raven's Roost (elevation 3200') is spread over 11 miles so the grades are not bad. There are short sections of **7%** but most of it is much less. This is also true south of Raven's Roost until you get near Yankee Horse Ridge (elevation 3140'), which is a few miles south of highway 56, where there is a southbound descent to Irish Gap (elevation 2279'). This is a little over **3 miles of 6 to 7%** descent (southbound). Between Irish Gap and the junction with US 60, the grades are not bad with the longest being 1¾ miles of 6% (southbound climb) just a few miles north of US 60.

Going south from US 60 there are some rolling hills and then a short climb. This point is about 3½ miles south of US 60 and is the beginning of a descent that is **4 miles of 7 to 8%**, the end of which is at Bluff Mountain Tunnel. South of the tunnel the grade eases down in short steep sections alternating with short sections of mild grade until you reach the junction with Virginia highway 130. This is the lowest point on the Parkway with an elevation of 649'.

Now, pay attention here folks. There is not much change in elevation between highway 130 (the lowest point on the Parkway) and US 501, but just south of 501 a southbound climb begins that takes you to the highest point on the Parkway (in Virginia) where the elevation is 3950'. This is a change in elevation of roughly 3300' spread over **12 miles for an average grade of just over 5%. Now, some of this is 6 to 7% and some is less than 5% but any way you slice it, this is a long hill.** If you are climbing this hill in the heat of summer it might be wise to unhook a towed vehicle or climb it early in the morning when it is cooler. If you are descending this hill there are overlooks where you can pull off and let brakes cool if necessary. There is enough 4 and 5% grade during the descent that you may not need to cool off the brakes, but as they say, better safe than sorry.

The southbound descent from the highest point on the Parkway begins with about **1½ miles of 7%**. From this point the grade stair steps down with short sections of 7% alternating with sections of mild or flat grade. This continues to just north of Powells Gap where the grade descends at a **steady 8%** for the last **1¾ mile** to Powells Gap. The last significant grade before reaching Roanoke begins about 5½ miles north of the junction with US 460. It starts with about **2½ miles of steady 7%** southbound descent. The last **3 miles** down to the highway 460 are short sections of **7%** alternating with sections of mild or flat grade.

BR The Blue Ridge Parkway *(between Roanoke & the North Carolina state line.)*

The longest grade on this section of the Parkway begins about milepost 133. This is the northbound descent toward Roanoke. It is about **4½ miles of 6 to 8%** grade with some 30 mph curves. After that the grade stair steps down with short sections of **7%** alternating with short sections of flat or mild grade.

Between milepost 133 and the North Carolina state line, there are many climbs and descents that may be as steep as **7 or 8%,** but they are seldom over a mile or two in length. It is a very pleasant drive on smooth two lane road. The speed limit on the Parkway is 45 mph.

1 Virginia highway 55 *(between I-81 and Wardensville, WV.)*

The summit of this hill is at the Virginia-West Virginia state line. The east side is about **4½ miles** of grade that is about **6%** during the top mile, then eases to 2 or 3% for a mile and then varies from **5% to 9%** during the last **two miles**, getting steeper as you descend. Between the bottom of this grade and I-81, there are rolling hills, some of which are as much as **9%** but not as long.

The west side of the hill is posted at **9% for 4 miles.** The upper 2 miles are **steady 9%** but the last 2 miles ease somewhat to about **7%.** This is a good two lane road with curves that range from 30 to 40 mph during the steep sections.

2 US highway 211 *(between Luray and Sperryville, VA.)*

The top of this hill is called Thornton Gap. The west side is about **4 miles of 6 to 7%** grade with many sharp curves and two 25 mph hairpin turns.

The east side is **4 miles of 7 to 8%** grade, also with sharp curves and two 25 mph hairpins.

3 US highway 211 *(east of New Market, VA.)*

The top of this hill is about 4 miles east of New Market on US 211. The west side of the hill is about **2 miles of 7 to 8%** grade with sharp curves and a **runaway truck ramp** about half way down.

The east side is **8 to 9% grade for 3 miles** with sharp curves. This is a good three lane highway with climbing lanes on both sides of the hill. There are school bus stops all along this road.

4   **US 33** *(between Harrisonburg, VA and Judy Gap, WV.)*

There are three summits along this stretch of US 33. The eastern summit is between Rawley Springs, VA and Brandywine, WV. The east side is **4 miles of 8 to 9%** grade. The west side is **4½ miles of 9%** grade and both sides have continuous sharp curves and hairpin turns. The highway is two lane on both sides.

The middle summit is between Oak Flat and Franklin, WV. The east side of this hill is **2½ miles of 8%** with 25 mph curves. The west side is about **3½ miles** of much milder grade. It is **4 to 5%** over most of its length. There are some sharp curves near the bottom. The road is two lane on both sides of the hill.

The western summit is between Franklin and Judy Gap, WV. It is **5 miles of steady 9%** grade on **both sides**. Both sides are two lane with sharp curves and hairpin turns. **Use caution on this road.**

5   **US 33** *(between Stanardsville and Elkton, VA.)*

This summit is known as Swift Run Gap. This is where US 33 crosses Skyline Drive. The east side of the hill is about **6½ miles** long. The upper **3 miles** are about **8%** with sharp curves and three lane road. There is a 1¼ mile break in the middle of the descent and then **2 miles of 6%** with 35 mph curves and two lane road. There is a **runaway truck ramp** about a mile from the bottom.

The west side is about **2½ miles of 8 to 9%** descent with 30 and 40 mph curves and three lane road. There is a **runaway truck ramp** about half way down the hill.

6   **I-64** *(east of Waynesboro, VA.)*

Rockfish Gap is at milepost 100 on I-64. This is where I-64 crosses Skyline Drive/Blue Ridge Parkway. The east side of this hill is about **5 miles of 5%** grade.

The west side is about **3 miles of 4-5%.**

7   **US 250** *(from the junction with highway 6 to Waynesboro, VA.)*

The east side of this hill is **3 miles of 6 to 8%.** The top of this hill is where highway 250 crosses under the Blue Ridge Parkway/Skyline Drive. The west side of the hill is about **2½ miles of 5 to 6%** and at the bottom of the hill you enter Waynesboro. This is good three lane road on both sides.

8   US 250 *(from Thornwood, WV to Staunton, VA.)*

There are a number of summits along this part of US 250. Starting from Thornwood, West Virginia and going east:

(1) This summit is at the state line. The west side is **3 miles of 9%** and the east side is **4 miles of 9%**. There are continuous sharp curves and hairpins on both sides.

(2) This hill is **1 mile of 9%** on the west side and **2 miles of 9%** on the east side. Sharp curves and hairpin turns on both sides. There are rolling hills through the valley before starting up the next grade.

(3) This hill is **2 miles of 9%** on **both sides**, again with sharp curves and hairpins. On the east side the grade continues right through the town of Monterey, VA.

(4) This hill is **2 miles of 7 to 8% on both sides** with sharp curves and hairpin turns.

(5) **Ditto the above.**

(6) **Ditto the above except only 1 mile on each side**. The east side of this hill bottoms out at the town of Head Waters, VA.

(7) This hill is **2 miles of 9% on both sides** with sharp curves and hairpin turns. The town of West Augusta is about 5 miles east of the bottom of this hill.

9   Virginia highway 84 *(just east of the West Virginia state line.)*

This hill is **1½ miles of 9%** on the east side with two 25 mph hairpin turns. The west side is only **½ mile of 7%**. It is a good two lane road.

10   US 220 *(north of Warm Springs, VA.)*

The 10 mile section of US 220 north of Warm Springs includes many short but steep climbs and descents. The last of these hills is also the longest and is about **2 miles of 7 to 8%**.

11   Virginia highway 39 *(east of Warm Springs, VA.)*

The top of this hill is just east of Warm Springs. The east side is about **3½ miles of steady 8 to 9%** descent followed by about a mile of 5% at the bottom. This is a two lane road with 45 mph curves. The west side is about **1¾ mile of 9%** descent with 25 mph curves and a couple of hairpin turns. The grade continues right to the stop sign at the T intersection with US 220 in Warm Springs.

ALSO:

Virginia highway 39 *(west of Warm Springs, VA.)*

As you leave Warm Springs westbound on 39, the first mile is **6%** descent. The grade then eases for almost 2 miles followed by a **¾ mile 9%** descent. Right after the bottom of that hill a climb begins. It is **2 miles of steady 9%** with 20 and 35 mph curves and a 15 mph curve at the top of the hill. The west side of the hill is **3 miles** of grade that varies from **5 to 8%** with 20 and 25 mph curves.

About 6 miles farther west there is a **1½ mile 8 to 10%** climb to the junction with highway 92 at the West Virginia state line. This grade includes 30 mph curves and a 10 mph hairpin turn. There is little descent west of the junction with highway 92.

12 US 220 (north of Covington, VA.)

About 5 miles north of Covington there is a southbound descent on US 220. The grade is **5 miles** long and there are short sections of **7 to 8%** with **5 and 6%** in between. There is a **runaway truck ramp** almost half way down the hill. It is a very short sand ramp. This road is mostly two lane with a few short sections of three lane and almost continuous sharp curves all the way down. The last ½ mile as you enter the edge of Covington is 8 to 9% descent.

The north side of the hill is only about **1 mile of 7 to 8%** grade.

13 I-64 (west of Lexington, VA.)

There is a summit at milepost 41, which is about half way between Clifton Forge and Lexington. The westbound descent begins with a warning sign stating: **"Steep grade next 5 miles."** It is **5 to 6%** descent. There is no warning sign going east. The grade is milder and spread over 8 miles.

14 Virginia highway 56 (between Steeles Tavern and Massies Mill, VA.)

As you turn off of US 11 onto highway 56 you will be greeted by a sign stating: **"This roadway not recommended for through trucks." We would recommend no vehicles larger than a pickup and camper.** This is due to steep grades and sharp curves. The curves are sharp enough and the road narrow enough that a large vehicle would find it very difficult to stay in the proper lane during the curves. In some places there is little shoulder before a sharp drop-off and vertical rocks on the other side making it impossible to swing wide in the curves.

After leaving Steeles Tavern eastbound, highway 56 descends in several very steep but short sections until crossing the river in the valley floor. The climb to the top of the hill is almost 4 miles in length with about **3 miles of 10 or 11%** in the middle and a **½ mile of 5 to 6%** on both ends. Highway 56 crosses under the Blue Ridge Parkway about ½ mile before the top of the hill.

The upper and lower parts of the descent on the east side of the hill are stair stepping descent with short steep sections (as much as **12%**) alternating with short sections of mild or flat grade. The middle part of the descent is fairly steady hill that ranges from **8 to 12% for over 3 miles. The total descent is almost 9 miles. Use caution on this hill.**

15 US 60 (between Buena Vista and Forks of Buffalo, VA.)

The top of this hill is where US 60 crosses under the Blue Ridge Parkway. The westbound descent toward Buena Vista begins with a warning sign: **"8% next 4 miles."** Truck speed limit is 20 or 25 mph based on the weight of the vehicle. The grade is **very steady 8% the entire length**. There are sharp curves and a **runaway truck ramp** about 3 miles down from the top with **1 mile of 8%** remaining after the ramp. The grade eases to about 4% as you enter the edge of Buena Vista.

The east side of the hill is much different. The entire descent is almost **8 miles.** It starts out about 4 to 5% and increases to about **9%** until you are about 1½ mile down from the top. The grade then varies from 5 to 8% for another 1½ miles including a few short flat spots. The next 2½ miles are either uphill or rolling hills until you come to a steep grade sign. The next **3 miles are steady 8%** descent with sharp curves. The grade eases to about 4% a mile before Forks of Buffalo.

This is two lane road. Beware of the curves. They are not individually marked and some of the sharper ones can sneak up on you.

16   Virginia highway 43 *(between Buchanan and Bedford, VA.)*

The top of this hill is about ¼ mile east of the Blue Ridge Parkway. The eastbound descent toward Bedford is **3 miles of steady 10 to 11% followed by ½ mile of 7%**. There are 25 and 35 mph curves on this two lane road.

Highway 43 and the Blue Ridge Parkway are the same road for almost 6 miles. During this stretch the grade rolls up and down and the longest hill is a **1¾ mile 8%** southbound descent that bottoms out at Powells Gap.

The westbound descent on highway 43 from the Parkway junction toward Buchanan is almost **4½ miles of very steep grade**. The upper **3½ miles are about 10%** with very sharp curves and several hairpin turns. It is a narrow two lane road. The last mile at the bottom of the hill is **6 to 7%**. **Use caution on this road.** There is a sign on I-81 that says **RV's and trailers are not recommended on this highway.**

17   Virginia highway 311 *(between I-64 and Roanoke, VA.)*

As you leave I-64 southbound on 311 there is a sign telling you of a low clearance ahead. There are side by side tunnels 2½ miles south of I-64. The southbound lane goes through a very narrow one lane arched stone tunnel that is marked 13' 2" in the center of the arch and 11' 11" on the sides. The northbound lane goes through a steel culvert tunnel that is marked 13' 7".

There is another low clearance about 6 miles farther south. It is a steel bridge marked 13' 3".

About one mile after entering West Virginia a climb begins. It is **3 miles of 7 to 9%** with continuous 25 mph curves and 15 mph hairpin turns. The top of the hill is the state line and you are back in Virginia. The southbound descent is **3½ miles of 7 to 8%** grade. The upper part of the grade is not as winding as the north side but farther down the hill there are 30 mph curves. The grade ends at the junction of 311 and 18 North in the town of Paint Bank, VA.

About two miles south of Paint Bank another climb begins. It begins with **1 mile of 7%** and then goes to **8 or 9%** for another **2 miles**. The upper part includes curves from 20 to 40 mph. The south side of the hill is almost **5 miles of steady 8%** descent with many curves from 20 to 40 mph. This grade ends about 5 miles north of New Castle. There is one more minor hill before reaching New Castle. It is only about ½ mile of steep grade on each side.

Just south of Catawba there is a summit that is **1 mile of 7%** on the north side and **2½ miles of 7 to 8%** on the south side. It is two lane with 35 and 40 mph curves.

18   Virginia highway 42 *(west of New Castle, VA.)*

This eastbound descent ends at the stop sign in New Castle where 42 meets 311. It is **5 miles of 7 to 9%** with three short breaks in the grade scattered along the way. There are sharp curves and hairpin turns. The west side of the hill is not really a descent but rolling hills. The road is all good two lane.

19   I-81 *(between Roanoke and Christiansburg, VA.)*

This section of interstate includes several climbs and descents that are about 5% and are **several miles** long.

20   **US 460** *(between Blacksburg and Newport, VA.)*
This divided four lane road includes two minor summits. The eastern hill is about **1 mile of 8%** on **both sides**. The western hill is about **1 mile of 8%** on the east side; **2 miles of 8%** on the west side.

21   **US 221** *(between Roanoke and Bent Mountain, VA.)*
This is a one sided hill, the top of which is about a mile north of Bent Mountain. It is a northbound descent toward Roanoke. It is **3¼ miles of 8 to 9%** grade with almost constant 25 to 40 mph curves. US 211 is a two lane road with a third lane during this steep section. The truck speed limit for the descent is 25 mph. (Between Bent Mountain and I-77 to the south, there are many climbs and descents on US 221, but they are seldom over 1½ miles long. They may be as steep as **8 or 9%**.)

22   **Virginia highway 100** *(between Dublin and Poplar Hill, VA.)*
This hill is about **1½ miles of 6 to 9% on each side**. There are sharp curves including a couple of hairpin turns.

23   **Virginia highway 8** *(between the Blue Ridge Parkway and Woolwine, VA.)*
This southbound descent begins just south of the Parkway. It is **3 miles of 8 to 9%** grade with 20 and 40 mph curves near the top and a series of very sharp 15 mph curves near the bottom. After the grade bottoms out near Rock Castle Creek, there is a short **7%** climb and then another mile of **8 to 9%** descent to Woolwine. This is good two lane road.

24   **US 58** *(between the Blue Ridge Parkway and Stuart, VA.)*
There are 5 miles of short but steep rolling hills between the Blue Ridge Parkway and the beginning of this southbound descent on US 58. At this point a warning sign states: **"9% next 6 miles"** and the grade begins. Almost a mile later there is a short break in the grade as you pass Lover's Leap Wayside. The descent resumes and is **steady 9% for the next 3½ miles**. There are **two runaway truck ramps**. Many sharp curves must be negotiated before reaching the first one. The curves then become less severe but the grade remains steady. The second runaway truck ramp is about ½ mile after the first. About a mile after the second ramp the grade eases but there is still more grade ahead. It ends about the time you cross the Mayo River. This is a good two lane road.

25   US 52 *(between Fancy Gap, VA and Mount Airy, NC.)*

If you are traveling south on US 52 you will encounter a large red sign stating: **"Vehicles over 8 tons prohibited."** This must apply to RVs as well as trucks. You can continue south on 52 long enough to get onto the Blue Ridge Parkway because the descent on 52 begins just after the Parkway entrance. If you want to go to Mount Airy you will need to take highway 148 over to I-77 and go south on it and then highway 89 to Mount Airy.

If you are under 8 tons, here is the description of the southbound descent on US 52. It is **4½ miles of 7 to 8%** grade with 30 mph curves and **two runaway truck ramps**. The runaway truck ramps are more like launching pads. They are about the length of two trucks, they slope upward, and then they end in mid air. There are sand piles to slow you down but......Just make sure you don't need them.

After the second runaway truck ramp, the grade eases to about 5% but the grade is not over. There are two more short sections of **7 to 8%** before the grade ends.

26   I-77 *(between Fancy Gap, VA and the North Carolina state line.)*

This southbound descent begins about milepost 7 on I-77, and ends just north of the North Carolina state line. It is **5 and 6% (mostly 6%) for 7 miles**. There are **three runaway truck ramps**. They all exit to the right and slope uphill and they show signs of use. There are also warning signs about possible strong crosswinds.

27   Highway 89 *(between Galax, VA and Lowgap, NC.)*

Highway 89 crosses the Blue Ridge Parkway about 8 miles south of Galax. At this point a southbound descent begins. It is **3½ miles of 7 to 9%** grade with 25 and 35 mph curves. The grade ends north of Lowgap, NC.

28   I-77 *(between Wytheville, VA and Princeton, WV (and US 52.)*

This section of interstate includes several climbs and descents that are about **5%** and up to **4 miles** long. In addition, there are often fairly long stretches of 2 or 3% tacked onto the end of these steeper sections. This makes for long climbs in hot weather.

There are two tunnels, each about 1 mile long. If you avoid tunnels you can use highway 598 out of Bluefield (going south from US 460) and then US 52 to Wytheville. It is a much slower route, the grades are steeper, and some short sections of the road are not very good. On the plus side, there is far less traffic. The climb out of Bluefield on 598 is about **2 miles of 8 to 10%**. The descent on the south side begins gradually and increases to about **8 to 9%** with 25 and 30 mph curves and a couple of 15 mph hairpin turns. This descent lasts about **5 miles**. About a mile before the grade bottoms out, 598 passes under I-77 and becomes US 52. There are several more climbs and descents before reaching Wytheville, the longest of which is **4 miles of 7%**.

29   Virginia highway 16 *(between Volney and Marion, VA.)*

This two lane road includes several climbs and descents. The grades range from **5% to 8%** but they short hills. The longest is about **2 miles of 6%** on each side of a hill that is not too far south of Marion.

30   US 58 *(between Damascus and Volney, VA.)*

This road is posted a few miles east of Damascus: **"RT 58 to Volney not recommended for trucks over 35' in length. Use I-81 or 16 to Volney."** This road is narrow and the sharp curves are endless. There are even hairpin turns on flat ground. There are climbs and descents, some of which are steep, but they are not long.

31   Virginia highway 16 *(between Marion and Bishop, VA.)*

Upon turning north on 16 from US 11 in Marion, one is greeted by a sign stating that through **vehicles over 35' in length are prohibited on highway 16.** Twenty miles north there is another sign stating that **vehicles over 30' in length are prohibited.** This is because the hairpin turns and very sharp curves on the mountains ahead cannot be safely negotiated by large vehicles. In many of the sharp turns there are vertical rocks on the inside of the curve that make it impossible to see if anyone is coming from the other direction and a large vehicle cannot make the turn without using both lanes.

The first mountain is between Marion and Chatham Hill. The south side is **3¼ miles of 8 to 9% grade** with continuous 25 mph curves and hairpin turns. At the top there is a speed limit sign for the north side that says: "15 mph next 3 miles." The grade on the north side is **8 to 9% for 3¼ miles.** The extremely sharp curves and hairpins are continuous for the first 3 miles.

After a few short but steep climbs and descents in the valley, the climb begins to the tops of the second and third mountains, both of which are between Chatham Hill and Tazewell. The first is **1¾ miles of 7 to 10%** on the south side and **3¼ miles of 8 to 10%** on the north side with very sharp, continuous curves and hairpins. Immediately upon reaching the bottom of this grade, the climb begins up the next mountain. The south side is **3 miles of 8 to 9%** with lots of curves. The north side is **1½ miles of 7 to 8%.**

The last summit before entering West Virginia is about 5 miles north of Tazewell. It is **1 mile of 7 to 8%** on the south side and **3 miles of 8%** on the north side with continuous curves and hairpin turns. The grade bottoms out at the edge of Bishop.

32   Virginia highway 80 *(between Rosedale and Lindell, VA (south of US 19.)*

When turning onto highway 80 east (which actually goes more south than east) from US 19 near Rosedale, one is greeted by a sign stating that **vehicles over 30' in length are prohibited** on this section of 80.

This road is quite narrow and has extremely sharp and steep hairpin turns. In some places the only shoulder is air. In other words, the edge of the pavement is the edge of the mountain. Most of the grade on the north side is **10 to 12%** and lasts about **2 miles.**

The south side of the hill is **3½ miles** of grade that varies from **7 to 10%** with continuous sharp curves and hairpin turns.

As you approach Lindell from the north there is a **1½ mile 7 to 9%** climb.

33 Virginia highway 80 *(between Rosedale and Council, VA (north of US 19.)*

After turning onto 80 west from US 19 there is an immediate **9%** descent for **1 mile** followed by short but steep climbs and descents until you are several miles west of Honaker. At this point a **1¼ mile 7 to 9%** climb begins that includes almost constant curves. The summit of this hill is also the Russell-Buchanan County Line. The descent on the west side is **3 miles of steady 7 to 9%** grade with very sharp curves and hairpin turns. As of this writing, the road is under construction and they are making some of the hairpins less severe but the grade probably won't change too much.

Even after the bottom of the steep grade is reached, the sharp curves and even hairpins continue beyond the town of Council.

34 US 19 *(between Hansonville and Holston, VA.)*

This section of US 19 includes a **3¼ mile 7%** southbound descent that begins at the Russell-Washington County line. There is little descent on the north side.

35 Virginia highway 72 *(between Georges Fork (near Clintwood) and Dungannon, VA.)*

Highway 72 between Georges Fork and Coeburn includes two summits. The grades on these hills are short, usually a mile or so, and range from **6 to 10%**. There are sharp curves and a few hairpin turns.

Between Coeburn and Dungannon there are two summits. The first one south of Coeburn is about **1½ miles of 7%** on the north side and less than **½ mile of 7%** on the south side before the road begins to roll up and down. The summit north of Dungannon is much different. There is a short grade on the north side and the descent on the south side begins with a couple of miles of mild grade and 40 mph curves. Then the grade becomes steeper, to **8 to 9% for 4 miles** with constant sharp curves and very sharp hairpin turns. There are a couple of short breaks in the grade but don't become complacent because the curves can sneak up on you. Stay awake even after the 4 miles of steep grade are over because there are two very sharp curves as you enter Dungannon, which is 2½ miles after the grade has eased.

Highway 72 between Fort Blackmore and Gate City is under construction as of this writing . It is presently a narrow, rough, and winding road. The longest grade on this section of 72 is the northbound descent into Fort Blackmore, which is about **2 miles of 7 to 9%** grade.

36 US 23 *(between Norton, VA and Jenkins, KY.)*

Just to the south of Norton there is a **3 mile 6%** descent for southbound traffic. There is a ½ mile break in the grade about 2/3 of the way down. It is a divided four lane highway.

About half way between Norton and Pound there is a **steady 2 mile 7 to 8%** descent for northbound traffic. This is four lane divided highway.

There is a summit at the Kentucky-Virginia state line. The south side is **2¼ miles of 7 to 8%**. It is divided four lane to the top of the hill where it becomes two lane as you enter Kentucky.

The north side of this hill is **2½ miles of 8 to 9%** grade with a stop sign at the bottom. There are 25 mph curves and a 15 mph hairpin about 1½ miles down from the top. This is the junction with US 119 south.

The Kentucky side of this hill is under construction at the time of this writing and will probably be three or four lane soon.

37   **Highway 160** *(between Cumberland, KY and Appalachia, VA.)*
This is a major league hill. The summit is at the Kentucky-Virginia state line. The Kentucky side of the hill is **5½ miles of 8 to 9%** grade. The Virginia side is almost **4 miles of 7 to 8%.** Both sides have almost continuous sharp curves and hairpin turns. The lower portion of the Virginia side is one hairpin after another and they are very sharp.

As of this writing, guardrails are being installed on some sections of the Virginia side. There are sections of this road where the shoulder is almost a wish and the drop-off is very long and steep. The Kentucky side already has many guardrails installed.

ALSO:

Kentucky highway 160 *(north of Cumberland, KY.)*
You will need some muscle in your bustle for this one because the grade is almost **2 miles of 12% or more on both sides** of this hill. It is a fairly good two lane road.

38   **Highway 68/38** *(between Appalachia, VA and Louellen, KY.)*
This summit of this hill is at the Kentucky-Virginia state line. It is **1½ miles of 8 to 9% on both sides.** It is a rather narrow and rough road with sharp curves and hairpin turns.

39   **US 58** *(between Jonesville and Duffield, VA.)*
A few miles east of Jonesville there is a **2 mile 7%** descent for eastbound traffic. It is two lane with 30 mph curves. The west side of this hill is milder grade.

Just west of Stickleyville there is a summit that is posted as **9% on both sides**. There is about **1½ miles** of grade on both sides. It is 3 lane with 55 mph speed limit.

The longest grade is between Stickleyville and the junction with US 23 at Duffield. The west side is **1¾ mile of 7 to 8%** with 40 mph curves. The east side is **steady 7 to 8% for 3 miles** and the two lane road has mild curves and 55 mph speed limit. There is a pulloff at the top for brake checks.

40   **Highway 70** *(from Striggersville, TN to Jonesville, VA.)*
This road includes about six or seven minor summits but major league curves and hairpin turns. All but two of the climbs and descents are 1½ miles or less in length. The two "long" grades are barely over 2 miles in length. The grades vary from **6 to 9%** and there are many sharp curves and many hairpin turns. The road is fairly good two lane except for a 2½ mile section immediately north of the Virginia-Tennessee state line. This section is extremely narrow with very sharp turns that you can't see around. A large vehicle must use both lanes to make the turn so there is a risk of a head on accident. Even if you creep around the turn, someone coming from the other direction may not be creeping.

41   **Highway 83** *(at the Virginia-West Virginia state line (between War, WV and Stacy, VA.)*
The east side of this hill is about **2½ miles of 7 to 9%** with continuous sharp curves and hairpin turns. At the summit the road rolls up and down along the ridge for almost two miles. The west side of the hill is also about **2½ miles of 7 to 9%** grade with sharp curves and hairpin turns.

42 US 119 *(between Ermine and Oven Fork, KY.)*

At the bottom of this grade, truckers are warned of narrow, winding road and steep grade next 8 miles. On the north side of this hill, the upper **3 miles** are **steady 8 to 9%** grade. There is a break in the grade (but not the curves) and then another mile of **9%** at the bottom. There are almost continuous 20 to 35 mph curves and a few hairpin turns.

The south side is **6 to 8% for 3 miles**. The road is a bit narrower and the curves are sharp.

43 US 421 *(between Harlan and Bledsoe, KY.)*

The south side of this hill is posted at **8% (parts of it may be 9%) for 3½ miles** with another ½ mile of 5% at the bottom. It is two lane with many sharp curves.

The north side is posted at 7%. The upper **2½ miles are steady 7%** grade with another **1½ miles of 5 and 6%** at the bottom of the hill. The curves are not as sharp on this side. Both sides are good two lane road. There is a rock quarry on the north side and heavy truck traffic is present.

44 Kentucky highway 80 *(west of Garrett, KY.)*

This hill has about **2 miles of 7%** grade on the east side and **1 mile of 5%** grade on the west side. It is four lane road.

45 Kentucky highway 402 *(east of Slade, KY.)*

This one sided hill is a westbound descent into the town of Slade. It is four lane road with about **3 miles of 6 to 7%** grade.

EASTERN
TENNESSEE

KENTUCKY

VIRGINIA

NORTH CAROLINA

SOUTH CAROLINA

GEORGIA

ALABAMA

Lafayette
Abingdon
Bristol
Boone
Mountain City
Shady Valley
Johnson City
Roan Mtn.
Bakersville
Mars Hill
Black Mountain
Asheville
Spartanburg
Greenville
Monticello
Albany
Corbin
Cumberland
Harlan
Pineville
Middlesborough
Jonesville
Kingsport
Striggersville
Rogersville
Greeneville
Erwin
Unicoi
Newport
Waynesville
Valley Hill
Tazewell
Thorn Hill
Bean Station
Mooresburg
Jefferson City
Gatlinburg
National Park
Great Smoky Mountains
Cherokee
Franklin
Hiawassee
Helen
Gainesville
Monticello
Oneida
La Follette
Lake City
Knoxville
Maryville
Townsend
Walland
Chilhowee
Tapoco
Suches
Dahlonega
Cookeville
Sparta
Crossville
Spencer
Smithville
McMinnville
Pikeville
Dunlap
Altamont
Dayton
Loudon
Soddy-Daisy
Signal Mountain
Chattanooga
Dalton
Calhoun
Rome
Viola
Manchester
Whitwell
Jasper
Sewanee
Sherwood
Monteagle
Bridgeport

Legend

Pass or grade locations
Interstate highways
US highways
Toll highways
State highways

Higher elevations — reds
Middle elevations — golds
Lower elevations — greens

TENNESSEE

1   **US 421** *(between Bristol and Mountain City, TN.)*
There are two summits on this section of 421. One is between South Holston Lake and Shady Valley. The north side is **3½ miles of steady 7%** grade at the top and a couple of miles of milder grade at the bottom. The south side is **2 miles of 7%** grade. Both sides have almost continuous 25 mph curves and an occasional hairpin turn.

Shady Valley is flat for about a mile between the two mountains. The north side of the mountain between Shady Valley and Mountain City is **3 miles of 7 to 8%** at the top and about **1 mile** of winding **5 to 6%** at the bottom. The south side is about **4 miles of 7 to 8%** grade and then a mile of lesser grade. Both sides have constant sharp curves and there are about a half dozen hairpin turns on each side.

2   **Tennessee highway 143 (highway 261 in North Carolina)** *(from Roan Mountain, TN to Bakersville, NC.)*
The summit of this hill is Carver's Gap, elevation 5512', and is also the North Carolina-Tennessee state line. The Tennessee side is **7½ miles of steady 7 to 9%** grade. It is a good two lane. There are sharp curves but they are usually a long way apart, so watch your speed.

The North Carolina side (highway 261) begins with **6¼ miles of 7 to 9%** with an occasional short section of **10%**. The grade eases at the town of Glen Ayre. About 3½ miles past Glen Ayre, the grade resumes at **8 to 9% for 1½ miles**. There are continuous sharp curves in this section. After a ¾ mile section of mild grade the last ½ mile into Bakersville is 6 to 7% with a stop sign at the bottom. **Use caution on this road.**

3   **Tennessee highway 107 (highway 226 in North Carolina)** *(from Unicoi, TN to Red Hill, NC.)*
The summit of this hill is also the North Carolina-Tennessee state line. The grade on the Tennessee side is **3 miles of steady 8 to 9%** with 30 mph curves.

The North Carolina side is about **2 miles of 8 to 9%** with 20 and 25 mph curves. It is a good two lane on both sides.

4   **US 19W** *(south from US 23 in Tennessee to US 19 in North Carolina.)*
"Warning to truckers-switchbacks next 6 miles-consider alternate route." This warning is an understatement. This is a terrible road. It is more like a back country lane than a US highway. The switchbacks are extremely sharp and the road is very narrow and rough. Avoid this road if possible.

5   US 23 *(north of Mars Hill, NC.)*

There is a summit about 7 miles north of Mars Hill. It is **2 miles of 9% on both sides**. The road is three lane on both sides and the curves are not sharp. Truck speed limit is 45 mph.

There is another summit at the North Carolina-Tennessee state line. The North Carolina side is **1¾ miles of 8%** and three lane road. The road becomes excellent four lane on the Tennessee side. The grade is posted at **6%** and is almost **5 miles** long. It is a **strong 6%** and there are **two runaway truck ramps**, the first of which is about a mile down from the top of the hill. The road curves to the left and the ramp exits straight ahead. It is long and uphill. The second ramp is 1¾ mile after the first and it exits to the right and is also long and uphill. The grade continues for almost 2 miles after the last escape ramp.

6   Highway 70 *(from Striggersville, TN to Jonesville, VA.)*

This road includes about six or seven minor summits but **major league curves and hairpin turns.** All but two of the climbs and descents are 1½ miles or less in length. The two "long" grades are barely over 2 miles in length. The grades vary from **6 to 9%** and there are many sharp curves and hairpin turns. The road is fairly good two lane except for a 2½ mile section immediately north of the Virginia-Tennessee state line. This section is extremely narrow with very sharp turns that you can't see around. A large vehicle must use both lanes to make the turn so there is risk of a head on accident. Even if you creep around the turn, someone coming from the other direction may not be creeping.

7   Tennessee highway 31 *(between Mooresburg and Sneedville, TN.)*

There are three hills on this stretch of road with the southern most hill having the longest grade. The south side of that hill is almost **2½ miles of 8 to 9%** grade with continuous curves and hairpin turns. The north side of that hill is only a little over a mile of **9%** grade.

The grades on the other two hills are 1¾ mile or less in length and vary from **6 to 9%** but they both have continuous sharp curves.

ALSO:

Tennessee highway 66 *(between Sneedville and Rogersville, TN.)*

This 25 mile section of road has a number of climbs and descents, a few of which are 2½ or 3 **miles** long. Most grades are in the **7 to 8%** range but a few of the shorter hills are extremely steep. There are many extremely sharp curves and hairpin turns scattered all along the route. There are a number of places where the road is quite narrow and there is little or no shoulder before nearly vertical drop-offs on the side of the road. **This route is not a good choice for large vehicles.**

8   US 25E *(between Bean Station and Thorn Hill, TN.)*

The Bean Station side of this hill is **3½ miles of 6%** grade that has two very short breaks. The **upper 3 miles are steady.** The Thorn Hill side is almost **3½ miles of 6%** grade with two ½ mile sections where the grade eases. This road is four lane on both sides of the hill.

9   US 441 *(between Cherokee, NC and Gatlinburg, TN.)*

Commercial vehicles are not allowed in Great Smoky Mountains National Park.

The summit of this mountain is called Newfound Gap and is also the North Carolina-Tennessee state line. The North Carolina side of the hill is about **8½ miles of 7 to 8%** grade. There are several breaks in the grade in the upper 2 miles but **the lower 6½ miles are very steady 7 to 8%.**

The Tennessee side is **13 miles** of grade that varies from **5 to 8%**. Much of the grade is in the 6% range but there are several long sections of 7 to 8%, especially in the lower 6 miles. There are two very short tunnels on the Tennessee side. There are 20 and 25 mph curves on both sides, which are not always marked. It is a good two lane road and the speed limit in the park is 45 mph.

The road to Clingman's Dome is at the summit of this pass. It is 7 miles from highway 441 to the visitor center at the end of the road. There is some 6 to 7% grade but it is not steady. It is a good two lane road.

10   Tennessee highway 73 *(between Gatlinburg and Townsend, TN.)*

Highway 73 intersects US 441 at the Sugarland Visitors Center just south of Gatlinburg. About 1½ miles west of the intersection, 73 begins a **2 mile 8%** climb and then a **1 mile 7%** descent. The remaining distance to Townsend is nearly flat but the curves along the river are constant and some are sharp.

11   The Foothills Parkway *(between Walland and Chilhowee, TN.)*

Some maps already show the Foothills Parkway between Walland and Wear Valley but as of this writing (Fall of '96) that part of the Parkway is not completed. The only finished section is between Walland and Chilhowee.

If you enter the Parkway from Walland the initial climb is **3¼ miles of steady 6 to 7%**. The next 2½ miles are mild descent or flat grade. Then another climb begins which is about **2¼ miles of 6%**. The next 3 miles are rolling hills and then the descent to Chilhowee begins. It begins with almost **4 miles of 6 to 7%** and then, following a half mile break in the grade, another mile of **7%**, and then a mile of mild grade to the junction with US 129 at Chilhowee.

12   US 129 *(between Chilhowee, TN and Tapoco, NC.)*

For the first 3½ miles south of the Foothills Parkway junction, US 129 is flat as it follows the Little Tennessee River. Then, abruptly and without warning, sharp curves appear and the road begins to climb up at about **6%**. If there were a champion for the world's curviest road, this road would be a contender. There are an incredible number of curves and hairpin turns over the next 11 miles. The initial **6%** climb is about **3 miles** long. The next 8 miles are short climbs and descents with the ever present sharp curves. At this point, the North Carolina state line is crossed and the descent is very steep. It is about **9 to 10% for 1½ miles**. It has sharp curves and hairpin turns, but not like the Tennessee side.

13   US highway 127 *(south of Crossville, TN.)*

About 12 miles south of Crossville, just south of the town of Big Lick, there is a warning sign for southbound traffic: **"7½% grade next 2.4 miles."** There is also a sign suggesting appropriate truck speed limits according to weight. The 7½% indicated may be an average grade, with parts of the descents a little steeper and parts a little less than 7½%. In any case it is all descent with 45 mph curves. It is a good two lane road with three lane during the steep grade.

14   Tennessee highway 30 *(between Pikeville and Dayton, TN.)*

There are about 6 miles of rolling hills along the top of this mountain separating the descent toward Pikeville on the west and the descent toward Dayton on the east.

The Pikeville side is **4 miles of 6%** grade. It is a curvy two lane road. The lower part of the grade is currently under construction (Fall of '96) and it is not readily apparent what the result will be. It may be three lane or four lane. They will probably take out some of the kinks in the road but the grade may not change that much.

The Dayton side is almost **3½ miles of 7 to 8%** grade that begins without warning. It is a higher speed, three lane road with 45 mph curves that can sneak up on you. Beware of the curves.

15   Tennessee highway 30 *(between Pikeville and Spencer, TN.)*

There is an eastbound descent from Mt. Crest to Pikeville that is **3 miles of steady 7 to 8%** grade with a series of 15 mph curves near the bottom.

About 16 miles west of Pikeville there is a westbound descent into a valley and then a climb to Spencer. The descent appears rather suddenly with 15 mph curves and **7 to 8% grade for 2½ miles**. The climb to Spencer begins with grade that varies from **5 to 8% for 2 miles** and then stair steps up another mile with short sections of steep grade alternating with short sections of mild or flat grade. There are sharp curves and hairpins in the lower part of the grade.

Just west of Spencer, highway 30 begins a descent without much warning. It is **3 miles** of grade that varies from **5 to 8%** with several 15 mph hairpin turns. Highway 30 is good two lane.

16   Tennessee highway 111 *(north of Spencer, TN.)*

Just north of Spencer there is a **3 mile 8 to 9%** descent for northbound traffic. It is an excellent 3 lane road during the descent but at the bottom of the hill the road narrows considerably.

17   Tennessee highway 8 *(south of McMinnville, TN.)*

About 7 miles south of the junction of 8 and 56 highways, there is a descent for northbound traffic that is posted at **8% for 3 miles**. This may be an average because much of the upper 2½ miles may be steeper. The last ½ mile is about 5%. It is a good three lane road with 45 mph curves.

18   **Tennessee highway 56** *(south of McMinnville, TN.)*

About 20 miles south of McMinnville there is a northbound descent that is **3 miles of steady 6 to 7%** grade with several 15 mph hairpin turns and numerous other unmarked curves. The speed limit on this hill is 35 mph.

19   **Tennessee highway 111/8** *(north of Dunlap, TN.)*

This one sided hill is a southbound descent toward Dunlap. The grade is **4 miles of 6 to 8%** with 35 and 45 mph curves. It is a good road, partly four lane and partly three lane during the descent.

20   **Tennessee highway 111** *(between Dunlap and Soddy-Daisy, TN.)*

About 6 miles southeast of the junction with US 127 (just north of Dunlap), there's a descent for northbound traffic on highway 111. It is posted as **6% for 4 miles.** It's a strong 6%. The road is excellent divided four lane during the steep section and excellent two and three lane south of there until you get near Soddy-Daisy where the road becomes four lane again. There is a **3 mile 7%** descent for southbound traffic as you approach Soddy-Daisy. There is a **runaway truck ramp** near the bottom.

21   **US 127** *(between Dunlap and Signal Mountain, TN.)*

This road includes a northbound descent toward Dunlap and a southbound descent toward Chattanooga that begins at Signal Mountain. Between the two descents are about 11 miles of rolling hills. The northbound descent is about **5 miles** in length. The first mile includes short sections of **6%** grade alternating with sections of mild grade. At this point there is a warning sign: **"8% next 4 miles."** This is a two lane road with 20 mph curves and, according to a sign that looks like it was erected by local residents, a "Deadman's Curve."

The southbound descent toward Chattanooga begins in the outskirts of Signal Mountain. The grade varies from **5 to 8% for 4 miles**. It is a curvy road that is sometimes two lane and sometimes three lane. There are two very sharp hairpin turns near the bottom.

22   **Tennessee highway 27** *(between Whitwell and US 127 (north of Chattanooga, TN.)*

The top of this hill is almost 7 miles east of Whitwell. The westbound descent toward Whitwell is **4¼ miles of 6 to 8%** grade. It is good two lane road but there are numerous unmarked curves and a couple of 25 mph hairpin turns.

Going east from the top of the hill, there are two miles of stair stepping grade where short descents alternate with short sections of flat or mild grade. Then the descent toward US 127 becomes **steady 7 to 8% for almost 4 miles**. It is good two lane with 30 and 35 mph curves.

23   **US 41** *(north of Jasper, TN.)*

US 41 includes a **3½ mile 7%** southbound descent into Jasper that ends right at the edge of town in a 15 mph school zone. This is a good two lane road with 40 mph curves.

24   **Tennessee highway 108** *(between Griffith Creek and Whitwell, TN.)*

This is a one sided hill which is a southbound descent toward Whitwell. The top of the hill is about 6 miles north of the junction with highway 28. There is no steep grade warning at the top. The upper mile of the hill is not steady grade. There are short steep sections alternating with short sections of flat or mild grade. The lower **4 miles are steady 7 to 8%** grade with a stop sign at the bottom of the hill as you enter Whitwell. It is a good two lane road.

25   **Tennessee highway 108** *(between Altamont and Viola, TN.)*

About 5 miles north of Altamont there is a northbound descent that is posted as **8% for 3 miles.** It is good two lane road with 30 mph curves.

26   **US 41** *(north of Monteagle, TN.)*

This is a **3 mile 7 to 8%** northbound descent from Monteagle. It is good two lane with constant curves and an occasional hairpin turn.

27   **US 41A/64** *(west of Monteagle, TN.)*

About 5 miles west of I-24 at Monteagle a westbound descent begins that is posted as **7% for 3 miles**. The grade is **steady** and there are 25 and 30 mph curves. These curves are sometimes widely spaced. Beware of letting your speed build between curves because they will appear suddenly.

28   **Tennessee highway 56** *(between Sewanee and Sherwood, TN.)*

This southbound descent toward Sherwood is almost **5 miles** long but it is not steady. There are sections of grade that vary from **8% to 6%** with sections of mild or flat grade in between. There are sharp curves and at least one hairpin turn near the top.

29   **I-24** *(at Monteagle, TN.)*

The westbound descent from Monteagle begins with a warning sign stating: **"Caution- steep mountain grade next 4 miles."** The grade is marked at 5% but it is a **strong 5% for 3½ miles.** Almost half way down there is a 45 mph curve to the right. The concrete barrier in the median shows considerable damage from vehicles that have not successfully negotiated this curve. There is a rest area at the top of the hill where one could stop and check brakes.

About two miles south of the junction of I-24 and US 64, (at exit 135) the east and west bound lanes of I-24 separate and go around opposite sides of the mountain. The eastbound descent begins with a warning sign stating: **"Caution-steep mountain grade next 4½ miles."** There is a truck inspection station at the top where there is also grade information. The grade is posted as **6% for 4 miles. It is a strong 6%.** Truck speed limit is according to weight. There are **two runaway truck ramps,** the first about 1½ miles down the hill and the second about one mile later. Both exit to the left. Since trucks are normally in the right lane on a hill like this, any truck needing to use the ramps will need to cross two lanes of traffic to do so.

The westbound climb up this same hill is almost **6 miles of 4 to 5%** grade.

30   **Tennessee highway 58** *(between Lookout Mountain and Chattanooga, TN.)*

This is a good two lane road with **2½ miles of 8½%** descent for northbound traffic. It is a curvy road with at least one 15 mph hairpin turn.

ALSO:

Tennessee highway 148   *(north of Lookout Mountain, TN.)*

This good two lane road includes two sharp hairpin turns and 35 mph curves. The northbound descent from Lookout Mountain is **2 miles of 8½%** grade.

31   Indian Grave Gap *(between Bakersville, NC and Erwin, TN.)*

This is highway 197 on the North Carolina side and highway 395 on the Tennessee side. The summit is near the state line and although we have not driven this road we understand the grade is severe: about **3 miles of 10-12%** on the east side and **4 miles of 7-9%** on the west side.

32   I-75 *(near the Kentucky/Tennessee state line.)*

This hill is approximately **4 miles of 5-6%** grade. It is a northbound descent toward the town of Jellico, Tennessee, which is very near the Kentucky state line.

33   Tennessee highway 297 *(west of Oneida, TN)*

We have not driven this road but we understand there are short but very steep (**12 to 13%**) descents into a river valley. The grades on both banks of the river are **1 to 1.5 miles** long with several switchbacks on both sides.

34   I-40 and US 70N *(east of Cookeville, TN)*

We have not driven this road but we are told that both I-40 and US 70N include westbound descents toward Cookeville. Both are about **3-4 miles of 6%** grade.

35   Highway 16 in Tennessee and highway 79 in Alabama *(This location is slightly west of the edge of our Tennessee map. Please consult an atlas for exact location.)*

We have not driven this road but we understand there is a **2 mile 10%** northbound descent toward Winchester, TN and a **2.5 mile 6-7%** southbound descent toward Scottsboro, AL.

36   Georgia highway 17/75 *(between Hiawassee and Helen, GA)*

We have not driven this road but we are told there is a summit about midway between Hiawassee and Helen. The southbound descent toward Helen is about **5 miles of 7-8%** grade with one or two switchbacks.

The northbound descent toward Hiawassee is about **4 miles of 7-8%** grade. All two lane road.

37   US 19 *(north of Dahlonega, GA)*

We have not driven this road but we understand there is a summit north of the junction of US 19 and US 129. The southbound descent toward the junction with US 129 is about **4 miles of steady 7-8%** grade with several switchbacks.

The northbound descent is about **5.5 miles of steady 5-6%** grade.

38   Georgia highway 60 *(between US 19 and Suches, GA)*

We have not driven this road but we believe there is a summit a few miles southeast of Suches. The southbound descent toward US 19 is about **5 miles of fairly steady 6-7%** grade. The northbound descent toward Suches is about **2 miles of 6%** grade.

NORTH CAROLINA

BR   The Blue Ridge Parkway in North Carolina.

The Parkway includes many short and sometimes steep climbs and descents all along its length. It also includes some long and steep climbs and descents. Sometimes it is mild rolling hills. One can often anticipate a grade near highway intersections because the intersections usually occur at low points or "gaps" along the Parkway. The Parkway is smooth two lane and the speed limit is 45 mph except in curves, which are not always marked. If you pick up a Parkway map at a visitors center, it will tell you some of the elevations along the road and you can have an idea of what's ahead.

Air Bellows Gap is near milepost 237 on the Parkway. There is a northbound descent from there to milepost 232 but it is not steady. There are sections of **6 to 7%** descent interrupted by short flat spots or short climbs.

Elk Mountain Overlook is near milepost 274. From this overlook there is a southbound descent to the junction with US 421 that is about **3 miles** long and has sections as steep as **8 or 9%**.

There is a **2 mile 8 to 10%** northbound descent as you approach the junction with US 421 at Deep Gap. The top of this hill is near milepost 278. The south side of the hill is milder grade and is not steady.

Chestoa View, elevation 4090', is near milepost 321. The northbound descent to the junction with US 221 at Linville Falls is about **3½ miles of 7 to 9%** grade with 30 mph curves. The southbound descent from Chestoa View is about **3½ miles of 7%** and then another mile of milder grade.

The junction of North Carolina highway 80 is near milepost 344 on the Parkway. Milepost 355 is near the turnoff that goes to the top of Mt. Mitchell, which is the highest peak east of the Mississippi. There are three long grades between these two points. Starting from Mt. Mitchell, the first grade is a northbound descent and is about **3 miles of steady 7%**. The next grade, which is a climb going north, is about **2 miles of 8 to 9%**. The third grade is a northbound descent, which ends at the junction with highway 80. It is about **5¾ miles of 7 to 9%** with a short break in the grade about 4½ miles down. There are three short tunnels during this last descent.

The climb from the Parkway to the top of Mt. Mitchell is about **4 miles** long. The first two miles are **8 to 9%**. At this point you pass the park office and the grade eases for a mile. The last mile to the top is **6 to 8%**.

The southbound drive from Craggy Gardens Visitor Center at milepost 364, to Asheville at milepost 385, is almost all descent. Craggy Gardens is at 5497' and Asheville is approximately 2000' so there is a descent of almost 3500' spread over 21 miles. There are sections of **6 and 7%** grade that may be several miles long but usually the steep grade is in shorter sections with milder grade or short climbs in between.

The southbound descent from the highest point on the Parkway, milepost 432 (elevation 6047'), to Balsam Gap, milepost 443 (elevation 3370') is an average grade of almost **5% for 11 miles**. **This is a long and steep hill**. Some sections will, of course, be more than 5% and some less.

The section of the Parkway that has the most long and steady grades is from Balsam Gap, milepost 443, to the southern end of the Parkway at milepost 469. From Balsam Gap, the southbound climb to Waterrock Knob at milepost 451 includes **7 miles of very steady 7%** grade. The southbound descent from Waterrock Knob to Soco Gap is **4½ miles of steady 6%**. The southbound climb from Soco Gap to Lickstone Ridge Overlook at milepost 459 is **3 miles of 5 to 8%**. The southbound descent from Lickstone Ridge to milepost 461 is **2½ miles of 7%**. And from about milepost 463 to milepost 469, the descent is **very steady 6 to 7% for 6 miles**.

77

1   **US 52** *(between Fancy Gap, VA and Mount Airy, NC.)*

If you are traveling south on US 52 you will encounter a large red sign stating: **"Vehicles over 8 tons prohibited."** This must apply to RVs as well as trucks. You can continue south on 52 long enough to get onto the Blue Ridge Parkway because the descent on 52 begins just after the Parkway entrance. If you want to go to Mount Airy you will need to take highway 148 over to I-77 and go south on it and then highway 89 to Mount Airy.

If you are under 8 tons, here is the description of the southbound descent on US 52. It is **4½ miles of 7 to 8%** grade with 30 mph curves and **two runaway truck ramps**. The runaway truck ramps are more like launching pads. They are about the length of two trucks, they slope upward, and then they end in mid air. There are sand piles to slow you down but......Just make sure you don't need them.

After the second runaway truck ramp, the grade eases to about 5% but the grade is not over. There are two more short sections of **7 to 8%** before the grade ends.

2   **I-77** *(between Fancy Gap, VA and the North Carolina state line.)*

This southbound descent begins about milepost 7 on I-77, and ends just north of the North Carolina state line. It is **5 and 6% (mostly 6%) for 7 miles**. There are **three runaway truck ramps**. They all exit to the right and slope uphill and they show signs of use. There are also warning signs about possible strong crosswinds.

3   **North Carolina highway 89** *(between Galax, VA and Lowgap, NC.)*

Highway 89 crosses the Blue Ridge Parkway about 8 miles south of Galax. At this point a southbound descent begins. It is **3½ miles of 7 to 9%** grade with 25 and 35 mph curves. The grade ends north of Lowgap, NC.

4   **US 21** *(between the Blue Ridge Parkway and Thurmond, NC.)*

The top of this hill is almost 5 miles south of the Parkway. The north side of the hill is about a mile of **6 to 7%** and then rolling hills to the Parkway. The south side of the hill is almost **4½ miles of steady 7 to 8%** grade with continuous 35 mph curves. There are several short sections of three lane highway on the south side.

5   **North Carolina highway 18** *(between the Blue Ridge Parkway and McGrady, NC.)*

If you turn south on 18 from the Parkway, there is a **1 mile 8 to 9%** climb to the top of this hill. The southbound descent is **5¼ miles of 8 to 9%** grade with constant unmarked curves. The grade is **steady** except for a half mile break near the top. This is a two lane road.

6   **North Carolina highway 16** *(between the Blue Ridge Parkway and Wilbar, NC.)*

Once again, turning south from the Parkway begins a long, steep descent. This grade begins right at the Parkway and is almost **6 miles of 7 to 9%** with 35 mph curves. Parts of this road are three lane. There are several very short breaks in the grade near the top but the lower part of the grade is **steady.**

7   US 421 *(south of the Blue Ridge Parkway.)*

This southbound descent begins right at the Parkway (at Deep Gap) and is almost **5 miles** of grade that varies from **7 to 10%**, with most of it in the upper end of that range.   At the time of this writing (Fall of '96) the upper 1½ miles are under construction. The old section is very curvy and the new section will take most of the kinks out but will not change the grade very much. The lower part of the descent is already four lane.

There are **two runaway truck ramps**. The first is 3 miles down from the top and the second is one mile later. Both ramps are sand ridges, and both are short. The first ends in mid air and the second ends abruptly against the hill. About ½ mile before the first runaway truck ramp there is a turnout where you can stop and cool brakes. The truck speed limit is 30 mph.

8   US 321 *(south of the Blue Ridge Parkway.)*

Going south from the Parkway, US 321 winds and climbs through the town of Blowing Rock. At the south end of town there is a warning sign: **"Steep grade next 8 miles."** The first **2¼ miles** of descent are **7 to 8%** with 25 to 35 mph curves and two lane road. From this point the road changes back and forth several times between two lane and four lane. The sharp curves remain through the four lane sections. The grade becomes variable for the next **5 miles** with sections that range from **5% to 10%**. There is a **runaway truck ramp** about 7 miles down from the top of the hill. It is a short sand ramp that ends abruptly against a hill. There are about **1¼ miles of 8 to 9%** descent after the ramp.

9   US 221 *(south of Blowing Rock, NC.)*

About a mile south of where US 321 and US 221 split, there is a warning sign for southbound traffic on US 221. **"Narrow, steep, winding road next 19 miles. Not recommended for vehicles over 35' in length."** If your vehicle is tall, watch for overhanging rock on the southbound side. Most of the grades along this road are short but the curves are almost continuous and very sharp and narrow. The longest steep section is a **1½ mile 8 to 9%** descent into Linville. (The top of this hill is near the entrance to the private road that climbs to the top of Grandfather Mountain. A fee is charged for this trip. Due to sharp hairpin turns, vehicles over 28' in length are not allowed.)

10   North Carolina highway 181 *(south of the Blue Ridge Parkway.)*

The first 4 miles south of the Parkway are short but steep rolling hills. At this point there is a warning sign for southbound traffic on 181: **"Steep grade next 11 miles."** This road is steeper than it looks. There are a number of places where the grade eases but don't let this fool you. Make a note of your odometer reading as you pass the steep grade warning at the top of the hill and be on your toes until the 11 miles are completed. The grade varies from **6 to 10% (much of it is 8 to 9%)** with sharp curves that are present even in sections where the grade has eased. The road changes back and forth from two lane to three lane several times. This is a very long climb for northbound vehicles, especially in hot weather.

11   **US 221** *(south of the Blue Ridge Parkway at Linville Falls, NC.)*
This southbound descent begins about ½ mile south of the Parkway. It is **4 miles of 7 to 9%** grade with constant curves. Most of the road is two lane and is somewhat narrow. There is a **runaway truck ramp** about 3¼ miles down from the top. It exits to the right and slopes up slightly. The bed is sand ridges with sand piles at the end. There is **9%** grade after the ramp and then the road stair steps down with short descents alternating with short sections of mild or flat grade.

12   **North Carolina 226** *(south of the Blue Ridge Parkway at Gillespie Gap.)*
There have been many large vehicle accidents on this hill, some including fatalities. If you are coming from the north there are warning signs and a pullout before you cross under the Parkway. The warning signs include: **"By law, all trucks except pickups and vans, next right."** This takes you into the pullout where there are more warning signs: **"Truckers, steep grade, sharp curves next 3 miles. Speed limit 15 mph. No fine or penalties for using escape ramp. 14% grade and sharp curves next 3 miles."** Other signs give advice such as starting down the hill in a low gear, not shifting gears on the way down, and use the truck ramp if you feel you are in trouble. There is a **runaway truck ramp** 1½ miles down from the top. There are two pullouts on the way down where you can stop and cool your brakes, one before the escape ramp and one after. The curves are very sharp. This is two lane road.   As you cross under the Parkway bridge, the signs ahead are not easily seen. The road forks immediately after the bridge. Highway 226 bears to the left.

13   **North Carolina highway 194** *(between Villas and Banner Elk, NC.)*
This is shown as a primary road on some atlases but.........it is, simply put, a terrible road, hardly fit for anything but farm tractors. As you leave Villas there is a warning sign: **"Not recommended for vehicles over 35'. Steep winding road next 4 miles."** This 4 mile stretch of narrow road and sharp curves takes you to the town of Valle Crucis where there is another sign telling you the next 4 miles are the same. Wrong. The first stretch was an inconvenience. The second stretch is one of those where you say *"If I had known it would be like this........"* It is incredibly rough, very narrow with extremely sharp turns, and **very steep grades. Avoid this road if possible.**

14   **North Carolina highway 261** (highway 143 in Tennessee) *(from Bakersville, NC to Roan Mountain, TN.)*
The summit of this hill is Carver's Gap, elevation 5512', and is also the North Carolina-Tennessee state line. The Tennessee side is **7½ miles of steady 7 to 9%** grade. It is a good two lane. There are sharp curves but they are usually a long way apart so watch your speed.
The North Carolina side (highway 261) begins with **6¼ miles of 7 to 9%** with an occasional short section of **10%**. The grade eases at the town of Glen Ayre. About 3½ miles past Glen Ayre, the grade resumes at **8 to 9%** for **1½ miles**. There are continuous sharp curves in this section. After a ¾ mile section of mild grade the last ½ mile into Bakersville is **6 to 7%** with a stop sign at the bottom. **Use caution on this road.**

15 **North Carolina highway 226** (highway 107 in Tennessee) *(from Red Hill, NC to Unicoi, TN.)*

The summit of this hill is also the North Carolina-Tennessee state line. The grade on the Tennessee side is **3 miles of steady 8 to 9%** with 30 mph curves.

The North Carolina side is about **2 miles of 8 to 9%** with 20 and 25 mph curves. It is a good two lane road on both sides of the hill.

16 **US 19W** *(south from US 23 in Tennessee to US 19 in North Carolina.)*

"Warning to truckers-switchbacks next 6 miles-consider alternate route." This warning is an understatement. This is a terrible road. It is more like a back country lane than a US highway. The switchbacks are extremely sharp and the road is very narrow and rough. Avoid this road if possible.

17 **North Carolina highway 80** *(at the Blue Ridge Parkway.)*

This is a secondary road included here in case you think it might be a better choice than highway 226. If highway 80 is not prohibited to large vehicles, it probably should be. The descent on the south side begins right at the Parkway and is almost **5 miles of very steep grade** and very sharp curves and hairpin turns. Some of the curves have vertical rocks sticking up within inches of the pavement and the curves are so sharp that a large vehicle would have a tough time making the turn without using both lanes.   You can't see if anyone is coming from the other direction because the rock is blocking your view.

The first **4 miles** down the hill are **8 to 10% or more** and the last mile is about **6 to 7%**. The sharp curves continue after the grade has eased.

The northbound descent from the Parkway begins with almost a mile of **9%** and then about a mile of **6%** through the town of Busick. This side also has sharp curves.

18 **I-40** *(between Black Mountain and Old Fort, NC.)*

By law, **all trucks except pickups and vans are required to stop** at the top of this hill and read the information posted about the eastbound descent ahead. The top of the hill is near milepost 67 just east of Black Mountain. The grade is posted as **5 miles of 6%. It is a strong 6%.** There are **three runaway truck ramps**, all of which are short sand beds with sand piles at the end. There is about a mile of grade left after the last escape ramp.   The westbound descent is about **1¼ mile of 6%**.

19 **North Carolina highway 9** *(between Bat Cave and Black Mountain, NC.)*

This road is a questionable choice for large vehicles. Parts of the road are not too bad, but some sections are extremely narrow with very sharp turns and hairpins. There are several climbs and descents on this road. The descent on the south end where 9 intersects 74A is about **1¾ miles of 7 to 8%**. The descent on the north end that takes you into Black Mountain is about **2½ miles of 6 to 7%**. This is one of those questionable sections. The other climbs and descents are 1½ miles or less in length, about **6 or 7%** grade, and very narrow and curvy.

20 US 74A *(between Fairview and Chimney Rock, NC.)*
This road is shown as US 74 on some maps and US 74A on others.)

Trucks over 13,000 lbs are not allowed on US 74A between Fairview and Bat Cave, which is a couple of miles north of Chimney Rock. The top of this hill is about 8 miles west of Chimney Rock. The east side of the hill is posted as a steep grade for **6 miles**. Most of the grade is **5 to 6%** with constant curves and a few hairpin turns. There are a few spots where the grade eases for a short distance. The 6 miles are over when you reach Bat Cave but there are a few more short 6% descents alternating with mild grade or flat sections for the last couple of miles into Chimney Rock.

The west side of the hill is **steady 6 to 7% for 2½ miles** with constant hairpin turns. The highway is rather narrow two lane on both sides of the hill.

21 I-26 *(east of Hendersonville, NC.)*
There is a **2½ mile 7%** descent for eastbound traffic that begins near milepost 31 east of Hendersonville.

22 US 176 *(between Saluda and Valhalla, NC.)*
Soon after leaving Saluda there is a **4 mile** descent for eastbound traffic. The first **3½ miles** are **8 to 10%** with continuous sharp curves. The last ½ mile is 4 to 5%.

23 US 25 *(at the North Carolina-South Carolina state line.)*
US 25 is four lane road with a **3 mile 6%** descent for southbound traffic. The top of this hill is near the state line.

24 US 276 *(between Brevard, NC and highway 11 in South Carolina.)*
As you turn south on US 276 in Brevard, the following sign greets you: **"Truckers-8% grade, 15 mph curves next 22 miles."** The top of this hill is about 2¾ miles south of the state line. The north side is not steady grade. After ½ mile of **8%** descent at the top of the hill, the grade stair steps down with short sections of 6% alternating with sections of flat or mild grade. This continues for 2 miles.

The south side of the hill is **very steady 8%** descent for over **6 miles** with constant 20 to 35 mph curves and 15 mph hairpin turns. This is good two lane road with some sections of three lane.

25 US 276 *(at the Blue Ridge Parkway.)*
As you turn north onto US 276 from Brevard, the following sign greets you: **"Truckers-9% grades, 15 mph curves, 4500' elevations next 30 miles."**

The descent on the north side of this hill begins right at the Parkway. It is **3 miles of 8 to 10%** grade with constant curves and hairpin turns. It is good two lane road.

The descent on the south side is **9% for 3½ miles** at the top and then, after a break in the grade, the road stair steps down with short sections of steep grade alternating with sections of mild or flat grade. These steep sections are usually about 6% but a couple of them are 9%. The road is very curvy all the way down the grade, and after the grade eases the curves continue as the road follows the river.

26   North Carolina highway 151 *(north of the Blue Ridge Parkway.)*

This northbound descent begins as soon as you turn off of the parkway. It is **4 miles of 9 to 10%** with continuous very sharp curves and hairpins, very narrow roadway, narrow shoulder, steep drop-offs, and no guardrails. **Not a good choice for large vehicles.**

27   North Carolina highway 215 *(between Bethel and Rosman, NC.)*

As you turn south onto 215 at Bethel a sign greets you: **"Truckers-9% grade, 15 mph curves, 5000' elevations next 34 miles."** The top of the hill is at the Blue Ridge Parkway where the vertical clearance is marked at 13' 0". The descent on the north side of the hill is **8 miles** long and varies from **6 to 9%, with most of it about 6%**. It is fair two lane with many curves.

The descent on the south side is about **6 miles of 8 to 9%** with many curves and some hairpin turns. It is good two lane road. The grade eases for about 4½ miles and then there are rolling hills with sharp curves and short, steep grades the last 6 miles to the junction with US 64 near Rosman.

28   US 178 *(south of Rosman, NC.)*

The following sign greets you as you turn south on US 178 from US 64 at Rosman: **"Truckers-8% grades and 20 mph curves next 17 miles."** There are climbs and descents all along this road from Rosman to the junction with highway 11 in South Carolina. They are from **6 to 8%** and can be as long as **2½ miles** but most are shorter. The curves are constant.

29   US 64 *(between Highlands and Rosman, NC.)*

This road is continuous short but steep climbs and descents and endless curves. It is also rather narrow.

30   North Carolina highway 107 *(north of Cashiers, NC.)*

About 6 miles north of Cashiers there is a **steady 3 mile 8%** descent for northbound traffic. The curves near the top are 45 mph but as you go down the hill they get sharper with a 15 mph hairpin near the bottom. The rest of this road, from Tuckasegee all the way down into South Carolina, is constant curves and short but steep climbs and descents.

31   North Carolina highway 28 *(south of Highlands, NC.)*

About 2 miles south of Highlands, highway 28 begins a **3 mile 6 to 8%** descent. Then, after a ¾ mile break in the grade, there are **3 more miles of 5 to 7%** but this part of the descent is not steady. There are several breaks in this section. The remaining 15 miles to the junction with highway 107 in South Carolina include short but sometimes steep climbs and descents. The entire trip from Highlands to highway 107 is constant curves, many of them unmarked and many of them very sharp.

32   North Carolina highway 106 *(between Highlands, NC and Dillard, GA.)*

The top of this hill is about 3½ miles north of the North Carolina-Georgia state line. The northbound descent begins with about a mile of **8 to 9%** grade and sharp, often unmarked curves. The remaining 4 miles to the town of Highland is a roller coaster ride with many short but steep climbs and descents and endless curves.

The southbound descent from the summit is a different story. It starts with about **½ mile of 10%** and then 1½ miles of rolling hills. From this point it is all descent, starting with **6 to 7%** grade for about a mile and then **9 to 10%** descent for the last **3 miles**. The last 2 miles of the grade are in Georgia and the road becomes three lane with continuous curves and a 15 mph hairpin at the bottom.

33   US 64 *(between Franklin, NC and Chatuge Lake.)*

There is a summit about 10 miles west of Franklin on US 64. It is posted as **3 miles of 8%** on the east side with **two runaway truck ramps**. Truck speed limit is 35 mph. It is a **very steady** grade. The west side is posted as **2 miles of 5%**.

At the bottom of that 5% grade a **1½ mile 7%** climb begins to another summit. The west side of this hill is about **1 mile of 8%**.

About 2 miles farther west there is a steep grade warning: **"7% next 3 miles."** It is closer to **4 miles** in length and some of the grade may be steeper than 7%. There is an additional **1½ mile of 5%** at the bottom before the grade is over.

34   US 64 *(between Franklin and Highlands, NC.)*

This road appears to have been built a very long time ago. **Large vehicles may want to choose another route.** As you pass through the Cullasaja Gorge southeast of Franklin, the road is extremely narrow with sharp curves and almost vertical drop-offs. In some places the shoulders are about one foot wide before thin air and no guardrail. Other sections have vertical rock walls on one side and short man made walls on the other with very narrow road in between.

There is almost **8 miles** of descent from Highlands to the bottom of the gorge, but it is not steady. There are short sections of **6 or 7%** alternating with sections of mild or flat grade. The curves are constant.

35   US 23 *(between Dillsboro and Franklin, NC.)*

There is a summit about midway between these two towns. The north side is **2 miles of 7 to 8%** and the south side is **3 miles of 8%**. Both sides have sand **runaway truck ramps**. It is a four lane road with 35 and 45 mph curves.

36 North Carolina highway 28 *(between US 129 at the Tennessee state line and Franklin, NC.)*

Trying to describe this road will make a person almost as dizzy as driving it does. The 9 miles north of Franklin are fairly normal. The next 47 miles to the junction with US 129 are constant climbs and descents and constant curves. The grades are often as steep as **8 or 9%** but they are seldom over a mile long. There are also a few short sections of **10 to 12%** grade near the Fontana Dam. As you approach the river crossing near the dam (from the south), the last 6 miles add up to a descent even though there are short sections of mild grade and flat grade and even one ¾ **mile 10 to 12%** climb in the middle of the descent. The last ¾ **mile** just before the river is **10 to 12%** descent.

37 US 129 *(between Chilhowee, TN and Tapoco, NC.)*

The first 3½ miles south of the Foothills Parkway junction, US 129 is flat as it follows the Little Tennessee River. Then, abruptly and without warning, sharp curves appear and the road begins to climb up at about **6%**. If there were a champion for the world's curviest road, this road would be a contender. There are an incredible number of curves and hairpin turns over the next 11 miles. The initial **6%** climb is about **3 miles** long. The next 8 miles are short climbs and descents with the ever present sharp curves. At this point, the North Carolina state line is crossed and the descent is very steep. It is about **9 to 10% for 1½ miles**. It has sharp curves and hairpin turns, but not like the Tennessee side.

38 US 19 *(at the Blue Ridge Parkway west of Waynesville, NC.)*

The summit of this hill is where US 19 passes under the Blue Ridge Parkway. The east side is posted as **9% for 3 miles**. It is a **very steady** grade.

The west side is posted as **7% for 6 miles** with constant 30 mph curves all the way down. This grade is also **very steady** and may be more than 7% in places.

39 US 441 *(between Cherokee, NC and Gatlinburg, TN.)*
Commercial vehicles are not allowed in Great Smoky Mountains National Park.

The summit of this mountain is also the North Carolina-Tennessee state line. The North Carolina side of the hill is about 8½ miles of **7 to 8%** grade. There are several breaks in the grade in the upper 2 miles but **the lower 6½ miles are very steady 7 to 8%.**

The Tennessee side is **13 miles** of grade that varies from **5 to 8%**. Much of the grade is in the 6% range but there are several long sections of **7 to 8%**, especially in the lower 6 miles. There are two very short tunnels on the Tennessee side. There are 20 and 25 mph curves on both sides, which are not always marked. It is a good two lane road and the speed limit in the park is 45 mph.

The road to Clingman's Dome is at the summit of this pass. It is 7 miles from highway 441 to the visitor center at the end of the road. There is some 6 to 7% grade but it is not steady. It is a good two lane road.

40 US 23 *(at the Blue Ridge Parkway south of Waynesville, NC.)*

As you pass under the Parkway going south on US 23 there is a steep grade symbol and warning sign that reads: **"7% max next 5 miles."** Very little of the 5 miles is 7%. Most of it is about **4%** with short sections of **6 or 7%.** There is a **2 mile 6%** descent as you enter Sylva.

There is little descent on the north side of the Parkway as you go toward Waynesville.

41 North Carolina 209 *(between Hot Springs and I-40.)*

There is a summit about 5 miles south of Hot Springs on highway 209. The northbound descent toward Hot Springs is about **3 miles** of grade that alternates between **6% and 3 or 4%.** The grade is not too steep but the curves are sharp and constant. The south side of the hill is about **1½ miles of 6 to 8%,** also with continuous sharp curves and an occasional hairpin turn.

About 6 miles south of Trust there is another summit. The north side of this one is about **3½ miles** of grade with 20 mph curves. The upper **2 miles are 7 to 8%** and the lower **1½ miles are 5 to 6%.** The south side is **steady 8 to 9% for 3 miles** with 25 mph curves and then a mile of **5%** with a stop sign at the bottom of the hill.

To continue south on highway 209, make a left at the stop sign and begin a climb that is **8 to 9% for almost 2 miles.** After reaching the top, the descent on the south side begins at about **10% for 1¼ miles** and then eases and stair steps down with sections of steep grade alternating with sections of mild grade. I-40 is about 4 miles south.

42 North Carolina highway 63 *(east of Trust, NC.)*

The top of this hill, known as Doggett Gap, is about 5 miles east of Trust, which is at the junction of 209 and 63. This is a **very steep** pass with many sharp curves and hairpin turns, especially on the east side of the hill. It is good two lane road.

The east side is **4 miles** of grade, much of which is **10 to 12%** with continuous sharp curves and hairpin turns. The bottom **1½ mile is 6 to 7%.**

The grade on the west side is almost **5 miles** long. The **upper 3 miles vary from 7 to 10%.** From there the grade eases to **6%** and then stair steps down to the junction with 209, with sections of 6% grade alternating with sections of milder grade.

43 US 25 *(between Hot Springs and Walnut, NC.)*

There is a summit just east of Hot Springs on US 25. The descent toward Hot Springs is about **2¾ miles of 8 to 9%** grade and ends at the edge of town. The descent on the east side of the hill is about **2 miles of 8% with a runaway truck ramp** about 1 mile down from the top. The lower portion of this grade eases to about 5% and ends at the junction with highway 208.

Just east of the junction with 208 there is another hill that is **2 miles of 5 to 7%** on the west side and about **1½ miles of 5 to 9%** on the east side.

44   US 23 *(north of Mars Hill, NC.)*

There is a summit about 7 miles north of Mars Hill. It is **2 miles of 9% on both sides**. The road is three lane on both sides and the curves are not sharp. Truck speed limit is 45 mph.

There is another summit at the North Carolina-Tennessee state line. The North Carolina side is **1¾ miles of 8%** and three lane road. The road becomes excellent four lane on the Tennessee side. The grade is posted at **6%** and it is almost **5 miles** long. It is a **strong 6%** and there are **two runaway truck ramps.** The first is about a mile down. The road curves to the left and the ramp exits straight ahead. It is long and uphill. The second ramp is 1¾ mile after the first and it exits to the right and is also long and uphill. The grade continues for almost 2 miles after the last escape ramp.

45   Indian Grave Gap *(between Bakersville, NC and Erwin, TN.)*

This is highway 197 on the North Carolina side and highway 395 on the Tennessee side. The summit is near the state line and although we have not driven this road we understand the grade is severe: about **3 miles of 10-12%** on the east side and **4 miles of 7-9%** on the west side.

46   Highways 281 and 107 *(near the North Carolina / South Carolina state line.)*

North Carolina highway 281 becomes highway 130 in South Carolina. We have not driven this road but we understand there are several hills that are as steep as **10% for 2 miles** between US 64 in North Carolina and highway 11 in South Carolina. Highway 107 is similar.

ADDITIONAL INFORMATION concerning grades.

Some readers have called to ask questions such as "What is a 6% grade? How do you define that?" We are not highway engineers but the answer is not difficult after you understand the concept. For every 100 feet of level roadway, a rise or fall of 6 feet would be a 6% grade. A rise or fall of 7 feet would be a 7% grade. A rise or fall of 10 feet would be a 10% grade, etc.

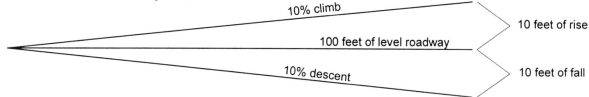

There are 5280 feet per mile so a 10% grade would be a rise or fall of 528 feet per mile. This would be 52.8 feet for each 1% of grade. The following table would result (with numbers rounded off).

528' of rise or fall in one mile is a 10% grade	
476'	9%
422'	8%
370'	7%
317'	6%
264'	5%
211'	4%
158'	3%
105'	2%
53'	1%

For example, Cloudcroft Hill in New Mexico is a 4315' change in elevation spread over 16 miles. This works out to an average of just over 5% for the entire 16 miles. (4315' divided by 16 = 270' per mile or 5+%.) This is a very difficult climb or descent because of the combination of length and grade.

READER INPUT concerning grades not included in earlier editions of this book.

As stated in the introduction, the area covered by *Mountain Directory* is so large that we probably missed some grades that deserve to be included in the book. If you have knowledge of such grades, feel free to write or call and let us know the approximate length, percentage of grade, location, highway number, direction of travel, and landmarks (such as towns or rest areas, highway junctions, mile markers, etc.)

Hills that are only a mile or two long probably won't be included because there are simply too many of them and they usually don't present a problem during descent because they are too short to cause overheating of the brakes. In most cases, the mountain passes and steep grades that we included in the first editions were those that are long enough and steep enough to be of concern to drivers of heavy vehicles during the descent. Generally speaking, any grades over two or three miles long and 5% grade or more are worthy of consideration.

The purpose of this book is to try to eliminate surprises for the drivers of heavy vehicles. Any information that makes mountain driving safer is welcome. If you have such information please write or call:

R & R Publishing Inc.
PO Box 941
Baldwin City, KS 66006-0941   **1-800-594-5999**